Truly
FEMININE

Truly FEMININE

DR. LINDA N. CAMERON

C iUniverse®

TRULY FEMININE

iUniverse books may be ordered through booksellers or by contacting:

iUniverse
1663 Liberty Drive
Bloomington, IN 47403
www.iuniverse.com
844-349-9409

Scripture taken from The Holy Bible, King James Version. Cambridge Edition: 1769; King James Bible Online, 2018. www.kingjamesbibleonline.org.

ISBN: 978-1-6632-2367-8 (sc)
ISBN: 978-1-6632-2368-5 (e)

Library of Congress Control Number: 2021910543

Print information available on the last page.

iUniverse rev. date: 08/18/2021

ACKNOWLEDGEMENTS

I began writing Truly Feminine in the 1970's when I was searching for some answers about my own femininity as I could not identify with the traditional feminist position espoused by Gloria Steinem and the Now gang at the time. Since the 1970's, I have updated the material twice and the current book was completed in 2021. As a result, the number of family and friends who have contributed to the writing of this book have grown significantly therefore I have divided the acknowledgements into several phases. The earliest phase of thanks goes to my parents. My mother, who provided a good model of the transformative feminine, taught me how to work to give form to my creativity while my father taught me about my inner Samson and Paul—my inner strength and reasoning abilities. This next phase occurs during the 1970's when the original manuscript was written. During this period of time, I had many religious mentors including Lorri Khoury and her father Chaplain Fremont Blackman, and Chaplain Frank Dickason and his wife Juliet who taught me during the crawling stage of my Christian understanding. Reverend Bill Littleton former rector of St. Paul Episcopal Church in Waco, Texas introduced me to Jungian Psychology and opened the door to relationships with Dr. James Hall and Dr. Flo Wiedeman, Jungian analysts in Dallas, Texas. Another mentor during this time was Luanne Klaras who taught me about creativity and how an idea can take many forms. During the final phase of my writing, I would like to thank individuals in my personal life particularly those in my weekly spiritual groups whose questions challenged me to refine my thinking about some of the ideas presented in this book. So here is a salute of gratitude to Rosalee Kinast, Pat Griffing, and Martina Griffing.

CONTENTS

CONTENTS

Chapter 1

FEMININITY TO MASCULINITY

> And the Lord God commanded the man, saying, Of every
> tree of the garden thou mayest freely eat: but of the tree
> of knowledge of good and evil, thou shalt not eat of it: for
> in the day that thou eatest thereof thou shalt surely die.
> Genesis 2:16-17

Traditional Christianity has interpreted the above scriptures as the fall of man following disobedience of God's command. But could this story also point to the birth of humankind's individual ego consciousness? In the beginning humankind lived in a state of unconscious oneness with God. Adam and Eve did not even know that they were naked but when they ate from the tree of knowledge of good and evil, their eyes were suddenly opened. Christianity focuses primarily on the split between good and evil that occurred in this fall, although our newly developed consciousness actually involves the awareness or perception of all opposites. In order to have consciousness, we have to have the ability to separate ourselves, a subject, from what we are observing and experiencing, an object. This notion is called the subject-object dichotomy and is spoken of in many Eastern religions. The belief here is that our spiritual journey in life is to transcend this split and reconnect with God in full conscious awareness rather than live in the original unconscious state of oneness with God. In the development of our consciousness we separated from God but our final relationship with God is one of actively and consciously choosing to be in an aware connected and loving relationship with the Divine. Isn't this a much higher state of being than that of unconscious identification with God. So, what is the ability we have that allows us to develop consciousness and an awareness of the world of opposites? God gave humans the gift of free will or the ability to freely will what we want with no limitations placed on its use and with this ability we freely separated from God. This separation involves a shift of our attention away from God to our own needs and desires and onto the world around us. We now become the king or queen of our kingdom. But unfortunately, when we shift away from God, we fragment our wholeness and unity and this gives birth to the world of opposites that we call ego consciousness. This book, *Truly Feminine*, focuses on one of these resulting opposites—namely the split between femininity and masculinity. It discusses how our newly developed ego can negatively impact these opposites within us as well as how to bring them back into balance so that we can again experience wholeness but this time with the addition of having conscious awareness of our wholeness and unity.

At the beginning of my spiritual journey, I focused my energies on understanding the feminine aspect of my being because I did not realize at this time that to be truly feminine involved reuniting the split between my masculine and feminine sides. I started my search by reading about the feminist movement. Books on femininity and women's issues reveal a diversity of viewpoints. Chris Beasley points out that feminism involves a number of social, political, economic, and religious movements centered around the issues of sexual inequality. The main idea is that women have been unfairly treated in patriarchal societies and efforts need to be made to undo gender stereotypes and establish opportunities for women that are equal to those of men.

In the western world, writers such as Maggie Humm, Rebecca Walker, and Prudence Chamberlain have divided feminism into four different waves. The first wave of feminism occurred in the late 19th and early 20th century and focused on getting women the right to vote. It is typically called the woman's suffrage movement and in the United States had such leaders as Susan B. Anthony, Lucretia Mott, and Elizabeth Cady Stanton who, according to Rosemary R. Reuther in *Women and Redemption: A Theological History* were influenced by the Quaker theological view that men and women are equal under God. This wave of feminism is considered to have ended with the passage of the 19th Amendment to the US Constitution, which granted women the right to vote in all states of the union. Although I am very happy to be able to vote as a woman, this wave of feminism occurred before my time, thus I have very little emotional connection to this trend within the feminist movement.

The second wave of feminism, called the women's liberation movement, began in the early 1960's and was dedicated to obtaining legal and social equality for women. Betty Friedan's 1963 book *The Feminine Mystique* is considered by Margalit Fox to have ignited the second wave of feminism in the United States. The NOW (National Organization for Women) was formed in 1966 and tried to get the Equal Rights Amendment (ERA) passed but never achieved this goal. Betty Friedman (President of NOW from 1966 to 1970) and Pauli Murray described the purpose of NOW as "To take action to bring women into full participation in the mainstream of American society now, exercising all privileges and responsibilities thereof in truly equal partnership with men." The Now Organization focused on six main issues including abortion rights and access to reproductive health services, domestic violence, constitutional and economic equality, racial diversity, and lesbian rights. Marches, rallies, lobbing, and conferences were employed to accomplish these goals. Women did gain reproductive rights during this time with the supreme court decision in the Roe vs. Wade case and reliable birth control medications. Now women were able to choose both a career and a family. In the United States, Gloria Steinem, often considered a liberal feminist, was a prolific author and activist during this time. She introduced to the American consciousness the activity of female genital mutilation in an article published in 1979 and concluded that men in a patriarchal culture used this to control women. I was in college and then graduate school during this wave of feminism and for all practical purposes appeared to be part of this movement of women out into the world. However, I could not identify with this movement because of my religious orientation and it seemed to me the feminists during this time were actually denigrating certain forms of feminine expression to the same degree that they were accusing men of doing. I could not accept the idea that I had the right to murder my own child and that such forms of femininity as being a homemaker were better than other forms of femininity.

A third wave of feminism began in 1992 and according to Charlotte Krolokke in her book *Three Waves of Feminism: From Suffragettes to Girls* was devoted to a focus on individuality and diversity. The beginning of this wave of feminism has been associated with Riot grrrl an underground punk movement in Washington state that combined the ideas of feminism with a punk style of anti-establishment views and Anita Hill's 1991 televised testimony of sexual harassment by Clarence Thomas, nominee for the Supreme Court. The second wave of feminism was criticized for focusing too much on the experiences of upper middle class women and set about bringing race related issues within the feminist movement. Debates among these feminists centered around whether there were innate psychological differences between the sexes or whether the observed differences were due to social conditioning. Other psychological issues addressed at this time can be found in the work of Georgette Mosbacher who talked about using her *Feminine Force* to overcome self-doubt and to gain her own power by becoming materially independent in the world. Gloria Steinem, in her book *Revolution from Within*, still blamed the patriarchy for her problems in being a woman in this culture. In *A Woman's Worth*, Marianne Williamson, who was a big proponent of *A Course in Miracles*, talked about anchoring her feminine worthiness in the eternal. Having completed my training as a psychologist at this time, I could readily relate to these issues as I was also actively searching for inner knowledge about myself and the true expression of my feminine nature.

The fourth wave of feminism began around 2012 and was committed to stopping sexual harassment, rape, and violence against women. This wave includes the 2017 and 2018 Women's Marches and the recent "Me Too" Movement in 2017 in which various women came forth accusing certain men in the public eye of sexual harassment and even rape in some cases. Forth wave feminists also focused on campus sexual assault and workplace harassment issues using social media technology such as Twitter, Instagram, Facebook, and You Tube.

This diversity of viewpoints and battling over what it means to be a woman and how to achieve the true expression of femininity not only left me feeling frustrated and confused but brought forth a number of questions in my mind. What approach best explains what femininity is all about? What approach will lead to the full actualization of the feminine side of one's being? Can an approach be found to extend the feminine principle in the world as we move forward and broaden the view of what it means to be feminine in the 2020's?

Whenever I run into varying viewpoints and theories regarding some issue in life, I remember D.E. Harding's concept of errors of omission. In his book entitled *Hierarchy of Heaven and Earth*, Harding states that in our search for truth we commit errors of omission. We see only fragments or opposites and fail to integrate these into a wholistic view of things. It is in this light, a wholistic view of femininity, that I began to focus my search. I wanted to develop a view of femininity that was inclusive rather than divisive. I then studied the works of such woman as Georgette Mosbacher, Gloria Steinem, Naomi Wolf, and Marianne Williamson who focused on identifying and undoing different blocks to their feminine development. It was at this time that I felt moved to use a Christian paradigm for several reasons. First, it seems to me that the average Christian woman in the culture and her views of femininity have for over twenty years been stereotyped and attacked by the more vocal, media-prominent feminists. I wanted to show that femininity manifests in many forms within the Christian tradition as illustrated in the lives of various women in the Bible. Secondly, books such as Dr. Este's, *Women Who Run with Wolves*, use stories and mythologies that most women in this culture have no connections with to illustrate aspects of feminine development. I wanted to use stories from the Bible as examples of femininity that the average woman in this culture could relate to and understand.

Like Mosbacher, Steinem, and Williamson, I began my search as a personal struggle to understand my feminine nature and its place in the world. However, the resolution that I found, though similar to theirs in some ways, turned out to be more wholistic and, I think, more inclusive of all women at differing stages of development of their femininity and in the expression of their particular form of femininity. It is to this search and its findings that I now turn.

For many years I struggled with doubts about my femininity. I felt as though I wasn't feminine enough. As a little girl, I wasn't particularly interested in dolls and went through a "tom boy" stage to my mother's dismay. During my later grade school years, I began to feel as though little girls were inferior to little boys. Reared in a small southern community within a Scottish family, I was exposed to the cultural reign of the patriarch. It seemed to me at the time that men and their approach to life were valued above women and their approach. I responded to this idea with anger since my prideful side didn't like being considered inferior because I was female. It also contributed to my doubts about the importance of femininity in the world. With the passage of time, I entered college and then graduate school. Doubts about my femininity during this period of transition increased as I watched all my girlfriends getting married one by one. I began to asked myself, "Why am I developing my intellect rather than getting married?"

In the midst of all these doubts, a strange thing dawned in my mind during my graduate school years. It all started with the advice I heard coming from individuals in the second wave of feminism or the women's liberation movement of the early seventies. It appeared to me that these women were advising members of their sex to give up being housewives, which they considered to be a secondary and an inferior role. "Come and join the masculine world," they seemed to be saying. At the time I was in school and for all outward appearances following this movement, yet not really, because there was something about all of this that disturbed me.

My first clue came in a phone conversation with my mother. I told her that a number of female graduate students seemed rather masculine, even in their body language. "If this is the way you have to be to get a degree," I told my mother, "then surely I don't want one." After hanging up the phone, I was both surprised and delighted at what I has said. In spite of the doubts that I had had for years, I was standing up for femininity. This puzzled me though because I didn't understand my feelings or behavior. I decided at this point to focus my energies on finding some answers, so I began what turned out to be a forty-year exploration of femininity and masculinity.

My search involved a number of questions. *What is femininity? How is femininity different from masculinity? Is femininity superior or inferior to masculinity? Should femininity be actualized or repressed?* I found that my question *What is femininity?* had been answered in four ways; these included biological, cultural, religious, and symbolic answers. The biological approach answers the question by means of the physical body. As Ann Ulanov puts it her book, *The Feminine in Jungian Psychology and Christian Theology,* "anatomy is destiny." An example of this approach can be found in the work of Sigmund Freud. Believe it or not, I was told by Freud that my femininity was due to penis envy. He saw feminine development as resulting from the lack of this prized organ. Somewhere between the ages of three and five, according to Freud, a girl realizes that she lacks a penis and comes to blame her mother for this. Consequently, she renounces the mother as her primary love object and turns to her father with the fantasy of possessing his penis. It's only when she transforms her desire for a penis into a desire to have a male child that she reaches maturity. Only then, according to Freud, does she become mentally mature.

The cultural answer to my question, What is femininity? can be seen in the early work of Margaret Mead. Mead regarded femininity as the traditional role that women have been forced into by a male-dominated society. Operating under this assumption, early feminists worked hard to bring about changes in our male dominated culture. They were helpful in opening up jobs for women that had traditionally been considered for men only and in taking steps toward more equal pay for women. Earlier cultural views of femininity can be seen in the writings of Gloria Steinem and what Dr. Christina Sommers calls "gender" feminists. These "gender" feminists have taken a left turn away from the mainstream feminist movement into the rather paranoid view that men are out for the humiliation and destruction of women. In *Who Stole Feminism?* Dr. Sommers points out that these feminists see women as being caught in a sex/gender system of male domination and victimization. They see humiliation and violence from men at every turn in the road. Dr. Sommers challenges the logical, factual, and scientific basis of many of the assertions of these gender feminists. She concludes that "how these feminist theorists regard American society is more a matter of temperament that a matter of insight into social reality."

The cultural approach maintains that there are no real differences between men and women except as created by male cultural standards. Lierre Keith in *"The Emperor's New Penis"* maintains that female socialization is a process of psychologically constraining and breaking girls—otherwise known as "grooming"—to create a class of compliant

8

victims. Femininity is a set of behaviors that are, in essence, ritualized submission. This appeared somewhat reasonable to me at first glance for I could remember my mother telling me that girls behaved this way and boys that way, particularly during my "tom boy" stage. Yet my mind traveled back in time to the first parents. Who taught them? I then went to Genesis 1:27 and found "So God created man in his own image, in the image of God created he him; male and female created he them." "Male and female created he them" suggests there are innate differences between women and men. I now seemed to have an answer as to how the first parents knew; it came from inside of them. These innate differences were then projected into role differences which became traditions for male and female behaviors. I was certainly glad to find that my femininity existed and wasn't just an illusion dreamed up and taught by society.

Since Christianity saved my femininity from nonexistence, I decided to look there for an answer to my question, *What is femininity?* What I found was hardly satisfying to me. Traditional Christian interpretations about masculinity and femininity told me that my femininity was inferior and subordinate to masculinity. Numerous scriptures were used to support this conclusion.

> Wives submit yourselves unto your own husbands, as unto the Lord. For the husband is the head of the wife, even as Christ is the head of the church: and he is the savior of the body. Therefore as the church is subject unto Christ, so let the wives be to their own husbands in everything. Husbands, love your wives, even as Christ also loved the church, and gave himself for it; That he might sanctify and cleanse it with the washing of water by the word, That he might present it to himself a glorious church, not having spot, or wrinkle, or any such thing; but that it should by holy and without blemish. So ought men to love their wives as their own bodies. He that loveth his wife loveth himself. For no man ever hated his own flesh:

but nourisheth and cherisheth it, even as the Lord the church: For we are members of his body, of his flesh, and of his bones. For this cause shall a man leave his father and mother, and shall be joined unto his wife, and they two shall be one flesh. Ephesians 5:22-31

But I would have you know, that the head of every man is Christ; and the head of every woman is the man; and the head of Christ is God. I Corinthians 11:3

Tradition has interpreted these scriptures as a chain of command in which authority passes downward from God to Christ to the Holy Spirit to man to woman and then, I guess, to children, cats, and dogs. At the risk of alienating some readers at this point, I must be honest in stating my feelings about this interpretation. This cosmic put-down of my femininity as secondary and inferior to masculinity left me feeling angry. But at the same time, I felt guilty for my angry feelings. If this was God's plan, then I should adjust myself to it. But how could love be so unequal? While still feeling a mixture of guilt and anger, I attended an Eve Reborn discussion group where this chain-of-command issue came up. I asked the following question: Suppose you are Bonnie and Clyde tells you to rob a bank? The answer that I got was yes, you should submit to this command. Maybe I'm just a rebel at heart, but this simply did not seem reasonable to me.

So far, my search to understand what femininity was had left me with penis envy, a stereotypical role conditioned by a male-dominated culture, a cosmic declaration that my femininity was secondary and inferior, and a command to be unreasonably submissive. Needless to say, at this point I was a little afraid to look further. More news like this would leave me with no other alternative but to hide my femininity behind a veil. While contemplating a veil of dark blue denim, which would extend from the bridge of my nose to the top of my toes, I discovered the symbolic answer to my question regarding femininity.

The symbolic approach was developed by Carl Jung and his students of Analytical Psychology. They challenged the prevailing cultural approach, which maintains that sexual differences are simply learned and that, given new cultural values, these differences would disappear. Instead, Jung saw both the feminine and the masculine as principles of the mind that one is born with. Thus, to be without sexual distinctions is to be without a part of the mind itself. These ideas corresponded well with those in the creation story, so I read further. Not only did I find answers to my question *What is femininity?* I found answers to my other questions. Let's look at how Jung and his students define femininity and differentiate it from masculinity.

According to Jung, the masculine and feminine principles can first be differentiated in terms of activity. The masculine mode of activity is of an initiating, arousing, erecting, and generating nature. It's asserting and moving toward some goal. This can easily be seen on a very biological level in the behavior of sperm, which flips its tail to initiate its movement to the ova. During the early part of the feminist movement, women were encouraged to identify with this aggressive, goal-oriented masculine form of activity. They were told to get out into the world, be assertive and develop career goals.

An example of masculine activity can be seen in a man's courting behavior. A man openly initiates a relationship with a woman who appeals to him. A woman, however, typically gets the attention of a man by subtle, more indirect maneuvers. Since the Clarence Thomas—Anita Hill Supreme Court hearings, "gender" feminists have labeled practically all male courting behavior involving this initiating masculine mode of activity as sexual harassment. On one college campus a procedure was developed in which men were required to get written permission from a date for each phase of physical contact. Although men have been harassed by the extreme feminists for their open and initiating courting behavior, women have been encouraged to take the initiative by calling men and asking them for dates. Isn't this strange? Masculine activity is attacked in men but encouraged in women.

In pursuing his goals, a man will actively change the environment and make consciously thought-out plans to achieve his goals. Once I experienced an extreme form of masculine planning. While in graduate school a group of friends and I decided to go backpacking during spring vacation. One of the guys on the trip was taking a course in backpacking, so we left all the planning to him. To my dismay, a printed itinerary was handed to me. Not only was the time for all meals rigidly set, the amount of time for cooking them was specified. After having lived under a rigorous graduate school schedule for several months, this did not appeal to me. The final straw came when my date and I were playing with the tents and hopping around like kangaroos in our sleeping bags. Our planner, or general as it now appeared, instructed us that such play was supposed to occur the first day of the trip. I looked at my date hoping my eyes communicated to him what I was thinking. I didn't mind being a WAVE in the sea, but not regimented like a WAAC in the army.

Some women have experienced such extreme planning during vacations with their husbands. Being a bit behind schedule, the husband may drive for miles without a pit stop. If you ask him to stop, he may accuse you of deliberately drinking that Coke four hours ago knowing that your bladder is only the size of a small green pea. It goes without saying, however, that this masculine mode activity is responsible for many achievements in our culture.

The feminine mode of activity, on the other hand, is defined as an open, receptive, and yielding attitude. It involves submitting oneself to a process, waiting and attending to things. This mode of activity is not merely passive as some people believe. It is simply a different kind of activity than that of the masculine mode. The extreme feminists have viewed this feminine mode of activity and its associated behaviors as inferior to the masculine form of activity. They have called on women to abandon the feminine mode of activity and particularly the traditional behaviors in which it is expressed such a baking and cooking.

The feminine and masculine modes of activity remind me of the kinds of activities involved in preparing a cake. The electric mixer with its rotating beaters reflects the generating and initiating activity of the masculine principle, whereas the mixing bowl that contains the batter reflects the feminine mode of activity. Its activity is containing and receiving, thus making it possible for the beaters to blend the ingredients. Biologically this mode of activity can be seen in a woman's reproductive activity. A woman must be open and receptive to the swimming sperm in order to achieve conception. The ovum awaits the penetration of the sperm. Then a woman must wait the nine months of pregnancy while the child is developing within her womb. Baking and cooking are behaviors based on an attending and waiting attitude toward food. Any woman who has prepared a turkey for Thanksgiving knows that constant attention and patience are necessary for the successful completion of this task. The behavior of waiting and attending to things often makes a woman appear to enjoy suffering. A man with his mode of actively changing a situation fails to understand why a woman adapts herself to the situation and waits for it to change.

Not only does the feminine mode of activity appear in the biological and behavioral spheres of a woman's life, it can be seen in the spiritual sphere as well. In fact, this feminine mode of open attentiveness and waiting would seem to be essential to having a religious experience. Just consider the many biblical passages that call for this waiting and receiving attitude.

> And therefore will the Lord wait, that he may be gracious unto you, and therefore will he be exalted, that he may have mercy upon you: blessed are they that wait for him. Isaac 30:18

> But if we hope for that which we see not, then do we with patience wait for it. Romans 8:25

> Behold, as the eyes of servants look unto the hand of their master, and as the eyes of a maiden unto the hand of her mistress; so, our eyes wait upon the Lord our God ... Psalms 123:2

> And the Lord direct your hearts into the love of God, and into the patient waiting for Christ. 2 Thessalonians 3:5

To experience the presence of God or the Holy Spirit, each of us must wait patiently and openly receive them into our hearts. Prayer also involves this form of feminine activity. For in prayer, we are opening ourselves to God, sometimes in contemplation and at other times to ask for help.

Another way that feminine activity can be seen in the spiritual sphere is in the principle of forgiveness. The feminine mode of "letting go" forms the basis of forgiveness. An example of the "letting go" aspect of forgiveness can be seen in Jesus' response to Satan's temptation when He was in the wilderness. Jesus said, "Get thee behind me, Satan." He did not defend against or attack Satan, Jesus merely let him and his remarks go just as light shines darkness away. In the process of letting go of things happening to us, we are recognizing and standing firm in our inner power given by God, which is more powerful than anything in the world or of Satan.

The differences between the feminine and masculine orientations to time has also been distinguished by Carl Jung and his students. The masculine mode of experiencing time is quantitative; that is, it is objective, clock-like and focuses on the past, present, and future. The feminine mode of experiencing time is qualitative rather than quantitative. Women experience time as subjective and personal; it is rhythmic, a waxing and waning. This rhythmical mode of feminine time can be seen in Ecclesiastics.

To everything there is a season, and a time to every
purpose under heaven: A time to be born, and a time to
die; a time to plant, and a time to pluck up that which is
planted; A time to kill, and a time to heal; a time to break
down, and a time to build up; A time to weep, and a time
to laugh; a time to mourn, and a time to dance; A time
to cast away stones, and a time to gather stones together;
a time to embrace, and a time to refrain from embracing;
A time to get and a time to lose; a time to keep, and a
time to cast away; A time to rend, and a time to sew; a
time to keep silence, and a time to speak; A time to love,
and a time to hate; a time of war and a time of peace.
Ecclesiastics 3:1-8

Here we see the ebbing and flowing of a personal time. The very
biology of a woman reflects this waxing and waning time rhythm. From
puberty onward, a woman goes through monthly biological changes
associated with her menstrual cycle. Her hormones shift from high levels
of estrogen to high levels of progesterone. This causes emotional and
behavioral changes to occur. Research indicates that during the last two
weeks of the menstrual cycle, progesterone, the hormone for pregnancy, is
at its highest level. Emotionally, this causes a woman to be moody, irritable,
and depressed. Today it is referred to as premenstrual tension or PMS.
A striking example of this syndrome came to me in a phone call from a
friend. She called me from Atlanta, Georgia and was just bawling. Since
this was a late-night, long-distance call, I just knew something terrible had
happened. When I finally had the nerve to ask what was wrong, she told
me that her garbage disposal had broken. Needless to say, I was stunned,
but I managed to tell her that I was sorry. "What's more", she said, "my
husband is still away, and the children are playing a game called Let's Get
Mommy". This game consisted of putting bubble gum on the light bulbs
to keep it soft while not in use, placing plastic wrap over the toilet seat
and dusting the furniture with oven cleaner. The last straw came when

the under-the-sink "jaws" went on the blink, and the water from the dishwasher backed up and spilled over on the floor. As we talked further, it turned out that my friend was under the tension of the last two weeks of her menstrual cycle, which made it more difficult for her deal objectively with the situation.

Other behaviors also change during the last two weeks of the cycle. A woman's activity level and taste sensitivity decrease while the amount of food that she eats increases significantly. But the next two weeks are a bit brighter for a woman. During this period, when estrogen reaches its peak level, a woman is very active and creative, and her taste sensitivity increases but her food intake decreases. Though some women throw these creative energies away in idle gossip, it would be wise to use this time for demanding tasks. Also, if you need to go on a diet, this would be an ideal time to begin because the desire for food is hormonally decreased.

A woman may attribute the behavioral and emotional changes associated with her menstrual cycle to the external world. It seems to her that external objects, conditions, and people change, thus causing her work to be easy at one time but difficult to complete at another. In reality, however, these changes are due to her inner rhythmical cycle rather than external conditions. To a man this cyclic aspect of a woman's nature is very puzzling. For example, in making decisions about some problem today, a man will, if external conditions don't change, follow his decided course of action the next day. That is, a man typically lives by an inner rational principle which says that if a thing is right today, it will still be right tomorrow. Thus, he expects that when a woman decides to do something tomorrow that she will do it. He fails to realize that a woman must consider not only external circumstances but, in addition, the changing character of her inner circumstances. To a man, a woman's dependence on an inner principle whose chief characteristic is change makes her seem fickle, inconsistent and unreliable. It is true that some women may arbitrarily change their minds for their own convenience or egotistical needs, but this does not alter the fact that cyclic change is an inherent part of a woman's feminine nature.

Some modern women have lost touch with this aspect of their feminine nature, a fact that has resulted in menstrual difficulties. Strong symptoms of physical or emotional disturbances during the last two weeks of a woman's monthly cycle may indicate a conflict between a woman's conscious attitude and the demands of her own nature. But if she recognizes her need to withdraw psychologically from the demands of external life and to live in the secret places of her own heart, she may re-establish contact with the deeper part of her nature and experience a healing effect. In *Woman's Mysteries*, Esther Harding suggests that the menstrual taboos upheld in primitive societies may reflect an unconscious knowledge of this aspect of a woman's nature. In Old Testament times, there were laws calling for the separation of women during childbirth and certain periods of the menstrual cycle.

> And the Lord spoke unto Moses, saying, Speak unto the children of Israel, saying, If a woman has conceived seed, and born a male child: then she shall be unclean seven days; according to the days of the separation for her infirmity shall she be unclean. Leviticus 12:1-2

> And the Lord spoke unto Moses and to Aaron, saying ... And if a woman has an issue, and her issue in her flesh be blood, she shall be put apart seven days: and whosoever toucheth her shall be unclean until the even.... But if she be cleansed of her issue, then she shall number to herself seven days, and after that she shall be clean. Leviticus 15:1-28

Men were even warned to stay away from women during this period of time.

> And if a man shall lie with a woman having her sickness, and shall uncover her nakedness; he hath discovered her fountain, and she hath uncovered the fountain of her blood: and both of them shall be cut off from among their people. Leviticus 20:18

> But if a man be just, and do that which is lawful and right, And hath not eaten upon the mountains, neither hath lifted up his eyes to the idols of the house of Israel, neither hath come near to a menstruous woman. Ezekiel 18:5-6

Modern men who have encountered the irritability and moodiness of women during these "unclean" times may wish such laws were still enforced today. Although I'm not suggesting a return to viewing a woman's menstrual cycle as unclean, it does seem reasonable that these Old Testament laws given to Moses point to a deep psychological need inherent in each woman's feminine nature.

Another observed difference between masculinity and femininity is in terms of their modes of understanding. The masculine mode of understanding is objective, head-centered, and analytical. Problems are solved by objectively viewing the pertinent facts then reaching logical conclusions from these facts. The technological complex in which we live today results from a scientific orientation that is based on this head-centered approach to life's problems. I have often pondered the notion that perhaps the legalism observed during Old Testament times reflects an extreme use of this mode of understanding. To gain salvation, one simply obeyed God's laws, the Commandments.

With Christ, we see a shift toward the feminine mode of understanding. Before examining how He emphasized this mode of understanding, let's define what it means. The feminine mode of understanding is heart-centered, subjective, and intuitive. An insight is conceived or born into the conscious mind without any awareness that a solution to the problem was being sought. You have probably experienced many instances of such realizations. For example, you just have a feeling that something is not quite right with your husband, your child or someone you know.

A retired chaplain and his wife, who are good friends of mine, once told me how they interrupted their vacation because of an intuition. They were stationed in Wurzburg, Germany shortly after World War II and decided to take off a couple of days to visit Italy. They spent in first night in Austria, which is about three hundred miles from the base in Wurzburg. The next morning, Juliet had such a strong feeling that something was wrong at the base that they turned the car around and returned to their home. Sure enough, the intuition was confirmed when they arrived. Frank, who was base chaplain, had to help with a difficult situation among some officers.

As you have probably guessed, the feminine mode of understanding is commonly called women's intuition. Men, who base their reasoning on the logical analysis of facts, often press women for the logical derivation they used to reach their intuitive conclusions. Women often respond that they don't know how they reached a conclusion but that they know that they are right. Many men, at this point, will ridicule a woman for not knowing how they know what they know. That such intuition is generally associated with women can be seen in the fact that in movies and plays women typically play roles of fortune tellers, tea readers and spiritual mediums. Even the Old Testament personifies wisdom as feminine.

> Doth not wisdom cry? and understanding put forth her voice? She standeth in the top of high places, by the way in the places of the paths. She crieth at the gates, at the entry of the city, at the coming in at the doors. Proverbs 8:1-3

> Wisdom crieth without; she uttereth her voice in the streets: She crieth in the chief place of concourse, in the openings of the gates: in the city she uttereth her words ... Proverbs 1:20-21

> Wisdom hath built her house, she hath hewn out her seven pillars: She hath killed her breasts; she hath mixed her wine, she hath also furnished her table. She hath sent forth her maidens: she crieth upon the highest places of the city ... Proverbs 9:1-3

That the feminine mode of understanding is heart-centered rather than head-centered can be seen in the following passages from both the Old and New Testaments.

> So that thou incline thine ear unto wisdom, and apply thine heart to understanding, Yea, if thou criest after knowledge, and liftest up thy voice for understanding; Yea, if thou seekest her as silver, and searchest for her as for hid treasures; Then shalt thou understand the fear of the Lord, and find the knowledge of God. Proverbs 2:2-5

> Who hath put wisdom in the inward parts? or who hath given understanding to the heart? Job 38:36

> My mouth shall speak of wisdom; and the meditation of my heart shall be of understanding. Psalms 49:3

> He hath blinded their eyes, and harden their hearts; that they should not see with their eyes, nor understand with their heart, and be converted, and I should heal them. John 12:40

Now let's look at how Christ emphasized using this feminine mode of understanding. In John 14:26, Christ says:

> But the Comforter, which is the Holy Ghost, whom the Father will send in my name, he shall teach you all things, and bring all things to your remembrance, whatsoever I have said unto you. John 14:26

It doesn't seem too far a step away to say that the feminine mode of intuitive understanding would allow us to focus on or open our hearts to the direction and guidance of the Holy Spirit. Such a focus allows the wisdom of the Holy Spirit to be born into our conscious minds.

Thus, in the work of Carl Jung and his students Ann Ulanov, Ester Harding and others, I could see what femininity was and how it was different from masculinity. It involved yielding vs. initiating activity, subjective vs. objective time perception, and heart vs. head understanding. At this point, I felt as though I was finally finding some answers to my questions. With further reading, I ran into the work of Edward Whitmont, another Jungian analyst, who categorized femininity and masculinity in terms of their dynamic aspects. Table I below presents an overview of his view of the dynamic and static aspects of masculinity and femininity.

STATIC MASCULINE

nonpersonal, objective,
reason, abstraction,
discrimination, law, order,
understanding, logical

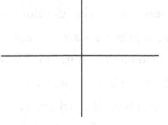

STATIC FEMININE	**DYNAMIC FEMININE**
inert, indifferent, impersonal, waiting, ceaselessly, creating and destroying, yielding, holding, containing, emotional, intuition	eros, urge to unite, unify, get involved with people rather than ideas/ things, emotional union, erotic involvement

DYNAMIC MASCULINE

drive, aggressive, battling,
challenging, conflict, will
penetrating, moving, urging,
striving toward a goal

With these Jungian ideas in my mind, I could see that both principles operated inside of me in varying degrees at different times. This realization did not startle me as much as Freud's notion of penis envy and it seemed in line with biblical scripture. Genesis 1:27 states, "So God created man in His own image, in the image of God created He him; male and female created He them. The statement "male and female created he them" suggests to me the idea that men and women are created to have both masculine and feminine qualities. I was already aware of this fact on a biological level; namely that my body contained both masculine and feminine sex hormones. Neurophysiological evidence had also suggested a separation of intuitive feminine functions and analytical masculine functions in the brain in terms of right and left hemispheric specializations. Our brain has two distinct hemispheres, a left and a right one. Research suggests that the left hemisphere is masculine and the dominant, talkative, analytical, and rational side of the brain while the right hemisphere is feminine and seems to be the more intuitive and perceptive side. Upon becoming aware that both the feminine and masculine modes operate within my personality, I felt my earlier childhood doubts of not being feminine enough fade away. A part of me did prefer to climb a tree or catch tadpoles in a ditch rather than play tea party with dolls. And this part was my inner man. But this did not mean that I didn't also possess a very feminine part.

I then began to read about the development of femininity and masculinity. Though both principles are present in our personalities, the feminine principle dominates in the conscious life of a woman, whereas the masculine principle dominates in the conscious life of a man. During the early phases of development both the girl and the boy are closely attached to the mother. Both then separate from the mother and identify with the father. This is typically called a "tom boy" stage in the girl's development. The boy identifies with the father and thereby the masculine principle. During this time of intense identification with the father, and learning to be a man, a little boy rejects his more feminine traits, his inner woman or anima according to Jung, but they remain in his unconscious mind. This rejection of the feminine principle can be seen in boys when they refuse hugging or tenderness and make fun of girls and "sissy" boys. Little girls have an added step in their development. They turn back to the mother and identify with her in order to internalize the feminine principle. Her inner man or masculine traits, termed the animus by Jung, then fall into the unconscious mind. Much psychological research has pointed to the importance of the mother in the development of both boys and girls, but this view of development underlines the importance of the father in development. Linda Leonard wrote an excellent book, *The Wounded Woman: Healing the Father Daughter Relationship*, which points out how a girl's relationship with her father can affect the development of her personality and relationship to men for the rest of her life.

When I finished reading about how girls and boys developed femininity and masculinity, I realized why I was disturbed by the second wave feminists as well as by the "gender" feminist of today. Though I agreed it was important to become aware of one's inner masculine side, I felt they were identifying with the inner man, or what Jungians call the animus principle, and throwing the baby of femininity out with the bath water. Possessed with the idea of developing the inner man, it seemed to me that they were throwing femininity out the window and, interestingly enough, like men in their early development, viewing femininity as negative and inferior. These "gender" feminists called upon women to reject their stereotypical view of femininity as tied to home and hearth. Gloria Steinem maintains that "societies ask us to play totalitarian gender roles." While teaching at a junior college, I talked with a number of women who were going to college for the first time and trying to develop their inner masculine sides. In the process of doing so they had thrown away their femininity, or at least repressed it. Their marriages were on the rocks because their husbands did not have the feminine principle to relate to in them and they had trouble relating in an intimate way to the masculine principle.

A second thing occurred to me while I was reading about how boys and girls developed their femininity and masculinity. My mind began to travel back in time to the creation story.

> And the Lord caused a deep sleep to fall upon Adam, and he slept: and he took one of his ribs, and closed up the flesh instead thereof; And the rib, which the Lord God had taken from man, made he a woman, and brought her unto the man. Genesis 2:21-22

Could the rib from which Eve was made be symbolically interpreted as pointing to an undeveloped or recessive masculine side, since it was taken from Adam? In a woman this recessive masculine side falls in the unconscious mind and the conscious mind identifies with the feminine principle. In a man the process is reversed. The masculine principle is actualized in the conscious mind and the feminine principle is in the unconscious mind. Also, the feminine principle or a man's inner woman, or what Jungians call the anima brings about his consciousness or tempts him into awareness. This also corresponds to the part of Genesis which states that Eve, his inner woman or feminine principle, tempted Adam to eat of the fruit of consciousness.

The idea of dominant and recessive femininity and masculinity did not strike me as strange for again I was already aware of this on a biological level. Though a woman has a predominance of female hormones, estrogen and progesterone, she also has recessive amounts of androgens, the male hormones. When the female hormones decrease during menopause, the presence of recessive male hormones may result in the development of facial hair. Also, some women who have been given androgens in the treatment of cancer may develop secondary male sexual characteristics. Men have a predominance of androgen but have recessive amounts of female sexual hormones. During later years, when the level of androgen drops, a man may show decreasing aggression. That is, while driving down the street behind a 20-mph speed demon, he may not express the desire to own a tank and dare anyone to get in his way as he goes 12 blocks in the wrong direction up a one-way street to get out of this one-car traffic jam. Though I was not surprised by the notion of dominant and recessive femininity and masculinity, in recent years, I have wondered if individuals who have transgender issues have merely encountered the feminine and masculine aspects of themselves. They have not realized each person has both principles within themselves and in the case of a man the masculine principle is dominant while the feminine side comes out more later in life when testosterone decreases. For a woman the estrogen-associated feminine principle is dominant, but when estrogen decreases during menopause, the testosterone-associated masculine principle becomes more dominant. It seems to me that psychologically integrating the masculine and feminine principles within oneself to produce a type of psychological wholeness is a much better resolution to this developmental issue than surgically removing one's genitals or being fixed in a transgendered state.

So far, I had found answers to the questions *What is femininity?* and *How is femininity different from masculinity?* But the question *Is femininity superior or inferior to masculinity?* remained. In thinking about the ways that femininity can be differentiated from masculinity—that is in terms of yielding vs. initiating activity, subjective vs. objective time perception, and heart vs. head understanding—I began to wonder whether questions of inferiority or superiority were relevant. Suppose, for example, you are planning to take a trip to Europe. No, you're not going as a port hole cleaner. This is a fancy trip and you can choose any mode of transportation. You find that two modes are available: plane and boat. One travel agency tells you that a plane is superior to a boat because it's faster. But saying that a plane is superior to a boat because it's faster is nonsense. A boat is not designed to fly at great speeds or, for that matter, to fly at all. It simply is not designed for that purpose. Spiritually, the issue of inferiority and superior is like asking whether Law or Love is the superior principle. They are simply qualitatively different and both should reign in the world in a balanced relationship. It may well be that Truth is an integration or marriage of the principle of Law with the principle of Love.

Like a boat and a plane, could femininity and masculinity be principles designed for different purposes in this life? And if designed for different purposes, can they be considered superior or inferior in those qualities for which they were not designed? Don't they, in reality, complement each other? If they complement each other in life, then how can one thing that complements and is complemented by another thing be viewed as superior or inferior to that thing? Rather, aren't both things necessary for a balanced relationship?

Could all of this be pointing to the fact that a man and a woman complement each other just as the head complements and is complemented by the heart? Consider for a moment that as women we show a natural tendency for a yielding and receiving type of activity—like the mixing bowl discussed earlier. This mode of activity complements the masculine mode of initiating and arousing activity—remember this was the electric mixer with its rotating beaters. There is a difference between openly receiving and thereby completing the masculine activity and submitting to and being dominated by the masculine. If the electric mixer dominated and forced submission on the mixing bowl, wouldn't the bowl be destroyed? There's a fine line here, but it's a very important one because relating through domination and submission involves superiority and inferiority. Such ways of relating can't be love for equality is gone. Yes, a woman is a helpmate to a man, but a man is likewise a helpmate to a woman. As a woman is the heart of a household, the man is head of the household, and both are necessary and important for a balanced relationship. The head is not superior or inferior to the heart, nor is the heart superior or inferior to the head.

I have often wondered if the view that women are inferior arises, in part, from the way a man develops his masculinity. As we saw earlier, during the development of their masculinity men typically reject their feminine traits, their inner women, and view this aspect of their personalities as negative and inferior. Unconsciously this negative attitude toward femininity gets projected outward onto actual women who are then seen as inferior and negative. Many women have suffered from such projections. While working at a women's shelter, I talked with many women who had been brutalized by their husbands. In most cases these men were extreme macho types who felt that women were inferior but who unconsciously were fearful of their own inner feminine traits, which they believed would destroy their masculinity and thus labeled them negatively.

To a lesser degree than battered women and in nonphysical ways the average woman in this culture has been subjected to this attitude of male superiority. Gloria Steinem and the women of NOW have simply attacked and blamed men for projecting this attitude of superiority and called on them to change. Although men do need to grow and change, women have a responsibility too because they have accepted the projection from men that femininity is inferior and have in some cases identified with the masculine principle.

The answer to the question *Should femininity be actualized or repressed?* seems to follow from the above discussion. If the feminine and masculine principles are both necessary for a balanced world, it may not be wise to depreciate or throw away either principle. A quick glance at our present cultural condition easily reveals the results of an imbalance between these principles in which the masculine principle dominates. I observed the effects of this imbalance in miniature form while working in a hospital pain clinic during my internship. In terms of the masculine vs. feminine modes of activity, practically all the patients were caught in the masculine mode. They showed an abundance of anxiety and tension in response to the striving, competitive, and changing world created by the domination of the masculine principle and its initiating and goal-directed form of activity. I used image relaxation to counter the effects of this domination. Relaxation involves the receiving, letting go mode of feminine activity. In essence, I taught the feminine principle of being rather than the masculine principle of doing. It's very interesting to watch patents when they first try to relax. They tighten their muscles and try too hard to relax. That is, they use their accustomed masculine mode of activity to accomplish the task. Of course, this only increases their tension. They soon learn that relaxation can be achieved only by shifting to the feminine form of activity—yielding, being, and letting go of the body.

I also saw this goal-directed, achieving, initiating masculine mode of activity emphasized in the physical therapy program for the patients. The important thing for the patient was to achieve a goal—time, distance, or mph on the treadmill or bicycle. These goals appeared more important than a patient's body or moving within the patient's bodily limits. This masculine approach to exercise can be seen throughout the culture. Many people today are involved in running and aerobics to the point of damaging their bodies to reach some goal or win some competition. Certainly, aerobics and the focus on its resultant cardiac conditioning is important for health, but there is a need to balance the masculine mode of exercising with the feminine mode of exercising. Ken Dychtwald in his book *Bodymind* presents an excellent example of exercising from a feminine mode.

Now, if I sit on the floor and try to reach over to touch my toes, I notice that I can only stretch about five inches away from my toes before I experience tension and slight pain. At this point, the muscles in my lower back and the muscles in the back of my legs are just too tight to allow me any further stretch. At this point I am experiencing one of my boundaries.

This point, or edge, is a highly important place . . . this edge is considered to be my creative teacher from whom I can learn about myself. If I approach this teacher/edge, with love, sensitivity, and awareness, I will discover that my teacher/edge, will move and allow me a greater range of motion. If I shy away from approaching my teacher/edge, I will learn nothing new, and in time my own dogma/tightness will contract upon itself and I will grow even tighter. If I try to blast past my edge, I might fool myself into thinking that I have learned and expanded, but in fact what usually happens is that I am only impressing myself with a temporary surge of ambition and that this feeling will probably contract upon itself with insecurity and fear, forcing me into greater confusion or potentially dangerous misunderstandings.

Here the body is not mistreated like a horse being whipped to reach some goal. The feminine mode of activity respects where the body is and gently bumps its limits to expand. In the past I was a student of the body method called the Alexander Technique under the instruction of Dr. Jim Hancock in the drama Department at Southern Methodist University. This technique is excellent in getting a handle on the masculine mode of activity. Alexander stated that we end-gain or focus so much on heading toward some goal that we contract muscles and misuse our bodies. Across time, such misuse damages the body, resulting in arthritis and in low back, shoulder, and neck problems. Alexander training helps focus your awareness on your body and on how to use it in a balanced, efficient manner. It teaches you how to extend and release your muscles in a free-flowing movement. This feminine mode of being, receiving and moving with the body can be used to your advantage when you are engaging in exercises, sports and other activities of daily living. The Alexander technique integrates the masculine and feminine principles in terms of bodily movement.

Another way in which I saw an imbalance between the masculine and feminine principles in miniature form in the hospital was in the methods of healing. Traditional medicine has primarily employed the masculine approach in the selection and training of doctors as well as in the types of techniques used for healing the body. Doctors are trained to be objective, analytical and scientific; that is, they are trained to use the left brain. They compete vigorously to get the highest grades in college so they can get into medical school. An assistant rector once told me that he was on a committee that was concerned about the personalities that this type of selection produced. Selection primarily on the basis of high grades resulted in students excelling in the left brain masculine activity of acquiring objective knowledge and in their having a very competitive attitude. But many such individuals became poor doctors because they related to their patients in a cold, clinical manner. They lacked the ability to use the feminine principle and could not establish a healing relationship with their patients.

The medical approach to healing is also saturated with knowledge derived from using the masculine mode of understanding. Medical doctors look at bodily disorders only in an objective, scientific way and feelings are kept out entirely. Treatments consist of external agents such as medications and surgical interventions to remove the enemy in our bodies; then everything is fine with the person. Now, I'm not saying that some conditions may not need this masculine approach to medical treatment, but why is the feminine approach left out or considered inferior? During my internship I used the feminine approach to healing and I still use it today. I don't use the penetrating scalpel to excise a problem that invades the body; rather, I view a bodily problem as a manifestation of feelings and emotional conflicts. Thus, the disordered areas can teach people what they need to look at, deal with, and change in their emotional response to heal themselves. For example, some ulcers in the stomach result from repressed anger, which causes the parasympathetic nervous system to become hyperactive. This hyperactivity results in too much hydrochloric acid in the stomach which literally eats the lining of the stomach wall. Needless to say, if the ulcer is bleeding, surgery may be necessary. That is, a more masculine mode of medical treatment may be needed or the person could die. But this treatment needs to be balanced with the feminine approach of dealing with the feelings which caused the ulcers.

The feminine mode of diagnosis and treatment can be seen in the image relaxation technique I talked about earlier. Images from the activity of the right feminine side of the brain can be used to diagnose what is causing a bodily problem. In one such guided imagery exercise, I take patients into a cave where an old wooden box is lying on the floor. This box, which is opened by patients in their imagery, contains an image of their pain. When the patients leave the cave, a person gives them another image, which will eliminate the pain image found in the wooden box. One male patient found a blob of protoplasm with waving hands all around it. When he left the cave, a woman was standing there and put a long black piece of rubber around his neck. The patient said that his neck pain immediately stopped when this happened in his imagery. After the exercise we analyzed his images to determine what they were symbolizing. The blob of protoplasm with waving hands was symbolizing his busy, controlling, workaholic side dominated by the masculine principle. The long, rubber-like substance placed around his neck by the woman, his inner feminine side, was pointing to the need of a more flexible, letting go attitude to reduce the pain in his neck.

Not only can a person's own imagery diagnose the problem causing a bodily disturbance, it can also heal the problem. Let me demonstrate how this works. Close your eyes and image a lemon. That is, call forth its smell, color, texture, size and shape in your mind and hold it there for a few seconds. Did you notice that saliva began to form in your mouth? If you did, you have a good experience of how imagery can change bodily function. Many people have been able to heal their bodies by using such imagery. They can slow down their nervous system, lower blood pressure, increase the activity of the pancreas, and change many other bodily processes without using medications. I've often wondered if our depending solely on the masculine approach to healing the body has prevented, or at least slowed down, the actualization of our inner feminine healing capacity.

A final way in which I saw an overbalance of the masculine principle during my internship was in the use of time. The important thing to be a good worker was to be on time. It didn't matter whether a person worked consistently during this interval of time. All productive, creative work had to occur during one's scheduled time. Anything occurring outside of the prescribed time did not count as work. One's body rhythm and periods of creativity were not considered at all. Again, the masculine principle of objective, quantitative time, dominated the feminine principle of a rhythmical flowing time.

The ascendancy of the masculine principle over the feminine principle can also be seen throughout our culture. Even within Christianity there seems to be more of an approach using the head or masculine over the heart or feminine approach. The charismatic movement that began about forty years ago reflected an attempt to emphasize the feminine principle of feeling, experiencing, and being in a personal relationship with Christ and God.

In miniature in my life sphere, I could see the fruits of the unbalanced relationship between the masculine and feminine principles. However, unlike Gloria Steinem and the "gender" feminists, I was able to avoid blaming and complaining. Instead, I realized the desperate need for the feminine principle in our culture—not a woman acting like a man, or trying to magnify her inner masculine principle exclusively, but a woman who truly magnifies the depths of her femininity. Our culture needs women who extend the feminine principle into every sphere so that it can join in a complementary relationship with the masculine there. Such a union between the masculine and feminine principles would truly result in a revolution throughout our culture. Similarly, a union of the masculine and feminine within our minds would result in a revolution and new stage of wholeness within each of us.

But now I was faced with a new question: *How to actualize the depths of femininity?* Again, I found the answer in the work of Jung and his students. Jung and his students maintain that for a woman to actualize the depths of her femininity, she must recognize and accept her inner man or masculine side. A woman should not become or identify with the inner men rather, she needs to recognize, accept, and transform these aspects of her being. Recognition or awareness of one's masculine side is the first step toward correcting his negative influence on femininity. Acceptance means that we are aware of the activity of our inner men but do not judge or condemn them; rather we take responsibility for placing and expressing them properly. Transforming our inner men or aspects of our inner masculine principle is a process whereby we direct our inner men away from carrying out our shadowy ego demands and then balance them with positive aspects of the feminine principle. Such acceptance and re-direction can result in our inner men becoming positive and serving our feminine values by extending outward into the modern technological world. If all of this seems somewhat paradoxical to you, then you are not alone because it certainly did to me when I first read about it. In the following chapters of this book, I will discuss the four aspects of every woman's inner masculine side and how he will work both for and against the positive expression of her femininity. I will also show how our inner men can be directed away from our ego needs and demands by balancing them with various aspects of our inner feminine side or so that we do not act out the shadowy aspects of our humanity and distort our femininity.

Chapter 2
MASCULINITY TO FEMININITY: SAMPSON

For years I have cooked, scrubbed, cleaned, sewed and chauffeured my family only to be deserted in the end. My son married some woman and moved to Oregon. The poor child is probably starving to death by now. My daughter left for college last week. I don't understand why she wanted to go so far away when there's a perfectly good college right here in town. And the man I married was a good husband until he got interested in his new hobby of sailing. The only real hobby he has is making a mountain out of a mole hill. He'll wind up drowning himself, and I'll become a widow and have to live all alone. Even the cat, which I nursed back to health after he was hit by a car, prefers to prowl the neighborhood rather than stay at home. What is a woman to do when she has been deserted by her loved ones?

*H*ow many times have you heard some version of this woman's story? Obviously, this mother can't let go of her husband, her children, or even her cat. Yet other women who are good mothers don't seem to have such difficulty in letting their family go. What's really going on inside of this Clinging-Vine Mother type?

> Why doesn't someone do something about the way people behave these days? I just read in the newspaper that three men and one woman robbed the cashier's office at the hospital. People should know that honesty is always the best policy: Their parents ought to have taught them that by the age of eight. And imagine, one of the thieves was a woman. Any woman should know that a hospital needs money to help people. They tell me that judges are too lenient on criminals. If were a judge, I would throw the book at them. No one should be allowed to get away with breaking the law.

Though this woman says, "If I were a judge," her whole conversation reveals that she has set herself up as a judge. Her reasoning is based on "shoulds" and "oughts" with no real examination of the situation at hand. Have you ever run across such a woman who moralizes and criticizes on the basis of unexamined dogmatic opinions? What makes some women behave this way?

> I can hardly believe what happened today at church. They elected Jane as chairman of the bazaar. She hasn't the slightest idea of how to set up a bazaar. Who does she think she is telling me that my ideas are not practical? I'm going to the rector of the church, and he'll see to it that I get what I want. I know I'm right. The bazaar will fail without me.

Why is this woman so upset that Jane was elected chairman of the bazaar? Why does she insist on being right and having her own way? Would she make a good boss or is she just bossy?

How wonderful! The bishop is coming to stay overnight with us. I must do something in his honor. A reception of some kind would be good. I'll only invite a few people from the church like the rector and vestry. Maybe I'll invite Charlene. I may need her help when I run for president of the Women's Association next year. Maybe I'll also invite Gail. She would probably like to come since she's trying to grow spiritually. But she's new in the community and not very well known. There's a lot I must do tomorrow, so I'll have to climb out of bed early.

The only climbing this woman is doing is up the social ladder. She doesn't show any real concern for the bishop at all.

So far, we have looked at four different types of women—the Clinging-Vine Mother, the Judge, the Boss, and the Social Climber. Though their behaviors appear different, these women do share something in common. They are all possessed by the same inner man or masculine dynamic, and he is distorting the expression of their femininity. Before we discuss each of these types of women, let's define this aspect of our inner masculine side.

This facet of a woman's inner man is collective, primitive, and power motivated. He provides a woman with strength, courage, and power to compensate for her outer feminine softness. Samson of the Old Testament is a good image for this aspect of our masculine side. Let's look briefly at the life of Samson so we can get a better feel for the characteristics of this inner man.

The story of Samson's life is found in the book of Judges. The period of the Judges was a time of transition. Israel had entered the Promised Land and settled in a world dominated by the Canaanite culture and religion. Under the leadership of Moses, Israel had been organized into a confederacy of twelve tribes sharing a common faith and grouped around a central sanctuary. Their God was Yahweh, who brought them out of slavery in Egypt and had entered into a covenant with them at Sinai. Their part in the covenant relationship was to be loyal to God and to keep his

Commandments. But Israel constantly fell into idolatry and then suffered at the hands of other nations. This is summed up throughout Judges in such scriptures as "the children in Israel again did evil in the eyes of the Lord," (Joshua 2:11, Joshua 3:7, Joshua 3:12, Joshua 4:1, Joshua 6:1, Joshua 10:6) and the "Lord sold them into the hands of the oppressor" (Joshua 2:14, Joshua 3:8, Joshua 4.2, Joshua 6:1, Joshua 10:7). But each time Israel failed Yahweh sends a judge to deliver Israel from the hands of her enemy. The Hebrew word "judge" means executor of justice, ruler, and helper. The judges were the forerunners of kings appearing between the time of Joshua's death and Samuel's rule. Somewhat like local governors, they exercised judicial functions over one or more tribes, led armies against the enemies of Israel, and protected the countryside from plundering nomads. Twelve men and one woman were raised up and designated as judges by God after Joshua's death. One of these judges was named Samson, which means "little sun." He lived during the time of Philistine oppression and gave his life to destroy these seafaring people who invaded the coastal strip of Palestine. Like the other Judges before him, Samson was a charismatic personality who showed feats of physical strength and prowess in war unequaled in both the Old or New Testaments.

> Then went Samson down . . . to Timnah . . . a young lion roared against him. And the Spirit of the Lord came mightily upon him... and he rent him as he would have rent a kid, and had nothing in his hand . . . Judges 14:5-6

> And Samson said, With the jawbone of an ass, heaps upon heaps, with the jaw of an ass have I slain a thousand men. Judges 15:16

> And Samson took hold of the two middle pillars upon which the house stood, and on which it was borne up, of the one with his right hand and of the other with his left. And Samson said, let me die with the Philistines. And he bowed himself with all his might; and the house fell upon

the lords, and upon all the people that were therein. So
the dead which he slew at his death were more than they
which he slew in his life. Judges 16:29-30

Thus, in the character of Samson we see not only a judge and ruler
carrying out the collective traditions and laws of the day but also a helper
who through the vehicle of primitive physical strength delivers Israel from
the hands of the Philistines. In a similar manner, within each woman is
a Samson. This "little sun" can provide her with inner courage, strength,
and power to face difficult situations in life. The Old testament character of
Esther seems to me to be a good example of the strength and courage that
our inner Samson can provide in our dealings with the world around us.

Esther was an orphan of great charm and beauty who had been reared
by a Jewish man called Mordecai. King Ahasuerus of Persia had put away
his queen, Vashi, for disobedience and was looking for another woman
to take her place. He ordered all the maidens of the land to be brought
to court for his inspection. Among the maidens was a Jewish girl named
Esther. At this time the Jews were being held captive in the land and were
a hated race of people. Mordecai made Esther promise not to reveal her
nationality. When King Ahasuerus saw Esther, he loved her above all the
other maidens and gave her the royal crown. About nine years after Esther
became queen, Harman, the prime minister, declared war on the Jews. He
ordered that all Jews were to be massacred on the fourteenth day of Adar.
Mordecai went to Esther and begged her to influence the king in favor
of the Jews. Fortunately for the Jewish people, Esther had not become
corrupted by her position of power and eminence. Rather, to save the
simple people from whom she sprang, Esther was willing to sacrifice not
only her position but also her life.

There was a law in the land that, under penalty of death, no one could
enter the king's presence unless the king extended the golden scepter as
a sign that she or he might advance to the throne. To save her people,
Esther had the courage to break this law by entering the king's presence

before he extended the golden scepter. "I will go in unto the king," she said, "which is not according to the law; and if I perish, I perish" (Esther 4:16). But when she entered, the king did extend the golden scepter and said, "What is thy petition? And it shall be granted thee." Esther told him that she had prepared a banquet for him and his prime minister, Harmon. On the second night of the banquets Esther revealed her nationality and told King Ahasuerus that a man had designs on her life and those of her people. "Who is he, and where is he, that durst presume in his heart to do so?" said the king (Esther 7:5). And Esther said, "The adversary and enemy is this wicked Harmon" (Esther 7:6). King Ahasuerus had Harmon hanged and reversed the order for a general massacre of the Jewish people.

In delivering her people from disaster, Esther stands as a real heroine. But the strength and courage she showed in this situation did not take away from her femininity. She was not judgmental, domineering, or aggressive in her manner. Instead, she was a mixture of feminine charm and strength. The very way that she chose to solve the problem appears to me to be more feminine than masculine. Esther remained loyal to her people and as queen was not driven by a thirst for power and eminence. She acted as an intercessor and loving mother figure for the Jewish people.

Now let's look at some ways our inner Samson, if unrecognized and misguided by the ego, can turn a negative face and distort the true expression of our femininity. Ann Ulanov in *The Feminine in Jungian Psychology and Christian Theology* suggests that in the Clinging-Vine Mother, Samson gets trapped in the mothering or maternal instincts. Thus, this type of woman is driven to mother in all situations. She lives for others but never develops her own unique personality. She relates to others in a collective way; that is, as husband, child, or friend rather than an individual personality. Though she supports her husband's career or position in the world, she ignores his personal qualities. Hence, her husband may come to feel that he is merely a fixture around the house and begins spending more and more time away with friends or with some sport. He may even become involved in affairs in order to assert his masculinity. In essence, the Clinging-Vine Mother type of woman relates only to a man's role in the world. She may become overprotective and possessive of her husband and children who no longer need her support. This may cause her children and husband to lack confidence in their strength and feel they have no right to exist apart from her mothering. This type of woman may have considerable difficulty later in life when her children leave home or her husband dies, unless she finds other ways to channel her unrecognized maternal instincts. It is important for the Clinging-Vine Mother type of woman to become aware of how her inner Samson is causing her maternal instincts to be distorted and harmful to others. She needs to recognize that her ego needs and demands are negatively affecting her inner Samson dynamic and thereby impacting the expression of her maternal instincts. With such an awareness, she can consciously choose to nourish, protect, and help in appropriate situations rather than be unconsciously driven to mother even when the situation does not call for it. I can remember once, when I first began doing therapy with people, having to control my mothering instincts. I gave so much to my patients in terms of working beyond my scheduled time late into the night that I wound up physically sick with the flu. During my illness, I realized how inflated I had become to think that I could endlessly mother everyone else and that, in fact, I needed to use a part of this energy to mother myself.

Another way that a woman's inner Samson aspect may turn a negative face and control her feelings and behavior can be seen in the Judge type of woman; here the inner Samson is split off from the feminine principle within and used negatively to meet perceived ego needs to be right, feel justified, and seek revenge. To understand what this means let's examine the dynamics of the woman called the Judge. Her inner Samson is not connected to the individual, personal, and subjective aspect of the feminine principle, but rather it operates on the basis of collective standards, general truths, and dogmatic preconceptions to which a situation must conform.

Thus, a woman's opinions reflect what may be true in a general way but don't really apply to the situation at hand. Her conversation is filled with "shoulds" and "oughts" and she doesn't consider the individual, personal situation. This aspect of Samson may get constellated during a marital dispute. When a woman perceives that she has been hurt emotionally, her inner man draws his sword to protect her. She will refuse to listen to reason and will respond to her husband's dismay with dogmatic opinions. The Pharisees can be thought of as representing this collective aspect of Samson. In the absence of any real personal religious understandings, they dogmatically applied their collective religious traditions to every situation.

> And he entered again into the synagogue; and there was a man there who had a withered hand. And they watched him, whether he would heal him on the sabbath day; that they might accuse him, ...and he saith unto them, "Is it lawful to do good on the sabbath days, or to do evil? to save a life, or to kill?" But they held their peace. Mark 3:1-4

A woman may direct her inner Samson's "should" and "ought" attitude inward onto herself, rather than toward the outside world. This may result in her feeling that she never does anything right or doesn't do enough. This notion of "shoulds" and "oughts" separates a woman in her relationships with others as well as in her relationship to herself. Such separation, whether externally in relationships or internally with one's self, is certainly not an expression of the feminine mode of connecting through love.

Another problem with "should" and "ought" thinking is that it leads to a judging, condemning, and blaming attitude. Judgment and condemnation lead to attack and revenge, which are considered to be justified, and this in turn leads to further attack, judgment, and revenge. In this ping-pong effect, the loving heart of the feminine principle is lost and separation between people increases. This same cycle can occur inside when we judge, condemn, attack, or take revenge on ourselves. In the story of Samson, we can easily see this cycle of events.

> And Samson went and caught three hundred foxes, and took firebrands, and turned tail to tail, and put a firebrand in the midst between two tails.
>
> And when he had lighted the brands on fire, he let them go into the standing grain of the Philistines, and burned up both the shocks, and also the standing corn with the vineyards and olives.
>
> Then the Philistines said, Who hath done this? And they answered, Samson, the son in law of the Timnite, because he has taken his wife, and given her to his companion. And the Philistines came up, and burned her and her father with fire.
>
> And Samson said unto them, Though ye have done this, yet will I be avenged of you, and after that I will cease. And he smote them hip and thigh with a greater slaughter: and he went down and dwelt in the top of the rock of Elam. Judges 15:4-6

This cycle of events constitutes what most people understand justice to be. But what a primitive sense of justice Samson shows in the above passage. Here justice and vengeance are seen as the same. But to be just is to be fair and not to be vengeful. Fairness and vengeance are impossible, for each one contradicts the other and denies that it is real. True justice is based on worthiness and not unworthiness. It involves the correction of errors, not condemnation and loss for anyone. Christ brought the answer to the problem of condemnation and revenge and its resulting unjust justice in the principle of forgiveness.

Judge not, and ye shall not be judged: condemn not, and ye shall not be condemned: forgive, and ye shall be forgiven. Luke 6:37

Many people misunderstand what Christ was really saying about forgiveness. They view forgiveness as giving unmerited pardon to someone who is guilty and unworthy merely to show that they are better because they forgive. The one you forgive is unworthy of your forgiveness, but you are being gracious by giving something undeserved. In this way of looking at forgiveness, you don't really gain anything directly by forgiving. What a distorted view of the principle of forgiveness that Christ introduced!

Forgiveness is really based on the "letting go" activity associated with the feminine principle. In fact, forgiveness means letting go of errors in oneself and others. Thus, the answer to judging and condemnation is forgiving—letting errors go. Christ called us to look past the errors of others to the image of God within them, for that is who they really are. Letting go of another's error also releases us from the error so that we can stay connected with the image of God or I AM Presence within us. In a way, judgment and condemnation focus on what is false in others and oneself—errors. Forgiveness, however, allows one to focus on what is true within each person—the image of God within.

In the principle of forgiveness introduced by Christ is the answer to correcting the negative inner Samson that is connected to one's ego needs and desires, which causes one to judge, condemn, and seek revenge. For Samson to function more positively, he needs to be disconnected from ego needs and desires using the feminine activity of letting go. For example, when a person finds that they are judging, condemning or seeking revenge in a situation, they should apply the Law of Forgiveness or the letting go form of activity associated with the femininity principle to these inner thoughts or external actions. In this way the feminine principle of letting go can be used to correct this aspect of the negative inner Samson.

Christ added another aspect of the feminine principle to help in the correction of effects of the negative inner Samson:

> But I say unto you which hear, Love your enemies, do good to them which hate you, Bless them that curse you, and pray for them which despitefully use you . . . But love ye your enemies, and do good, and lend, hoping for nothing again; and your reward shall be great, and ye shall be the children of the Highest: for he is kind unto the unthankful and to the evil. Luke 6:27-35

According to these words, love, the heart of the feminine principle, should be added to the principle of forgiveness. Again, we see the call back to the feminine to undo the negative, unbalanced masculine.

Let's examine why love should be given back in response to another's error. Consider for a moment someone's verbal attack. Behind the attack is anger and underneath anger is hurt. Many people profess that they are only angry, but always under anger is hurt. Basically, there are three ways in which we can perceive that we have been hurt. We can perceive that we have been hurt through the loss of love, the loss of power, and the loss of self-esteem. And what heals hurt but love? Thus, all behavior is either a call for love or an expression of love from the Holy Spirit or image of God within us. A person's angry verbal attack is really a call for love. Christ saw this call for love and was not put off by the form it took. This is why he called us to answer attack of any kind with forgiveness and love. Forgiveness means letting go of another's error and seeing the underlying call for love. Judgment and condemnation are really disguises for our failure to answer a call for love with love. Christ demonstrated perfectly how to handle attack with forgiveness and love at His crucifixion. He looked through the errors of His crucifiers and said "Forgive them, they know not what they do." He did not condemn, attack, or seek revenge. Condemnation and revenge reflect negative Samson's primitive sense of justice, which separates people and destroys love and further isolates us

44

from the feminine principle. Unlike Samson, Christ shows us what true justice is and how to achieve it. He uses forgiveness and love, the core aspects of the feminine principle.

Dr. Valentis and Dr. Devane, in their book *Female Rage*, state that women should allow themselves to become aware of their anger and rage so that they can "let it go." "Forgiveness follows when we choose to close those painful episodes in our lives and slip off rage like a dress that doesn't fit us anymore." "When a woman holds onto her rage, it becomes a poison circulating in her bloodstream; when she transforms it, rage can become determination, creativity, courage, and passion." These authors seem to be saying that anger can be transformed into determination, creativity, courage, and passion. Rather than being transformed into these positive characteristics, it seems to me that these qualities simply emerge when a person lets go of the rage blocking them out of consciousness. That is, our ego needs and demands block the presence of the "image of God within us" and thus these qualities cannot come forth. These authors then state that "rage is an emotion no woman can control; what she can learn to control is her behavior and response." They further state that the "wide breach remains between an ideal world of sexual equality and the realities of women's lives." "Female rage is created by this chasm and swirls in orchestra the fire, between expectations that raise hope and the real world that makes us see red." In order for these statements to be true, a woman would have to be a mindless puppet pulled into a raging dance by the strings of the external world. In this case, the external world of sexual inequality is the puppeteer. The statements of Valentis and Devane actually denigrate or attack the inner power of a woman, for they imply that the external world is controlling her. They shift her focus of power to an external origin when they say that it is the "real world that makes us see red." It also follows that the solution to the problem of rage lies in changing the external world. This kind of thinking, though prevalent in the culture, can lead to a victimization mentality and a "seek but do not find" philosophy of problem solving. As stated earlier, anger comes when we perceive in our minds that we have been hurt. We feel hurt by the external world when our minds take things said or done outside of ourselves and bring them into our minds in the form of a mental attack against us. We use or rather misuse the power of our minds to mentally attack ourselves over things said or done outside of us. Because our minds are so powerful, if we use them to attack ourselves with hurtful ideas, then we will feel hurt or weakened in some way. This mental habit of attacking ourselves with ideas that result in feelings of hurt has been so well practiced that it is an unconscious part of our behavior. We forget that we have attacked ourselves and blame the external world of people and things as doing it to us. We never learned the childhood song: "Sticks and stones may break my bones but words will never hurt me." By becoming aware of the way that we produce anger in ourselves, we can truly resolve our problems with anger and rage. Awareness that we are attacking ourselves mentally and then blaming others for it typically results in a choice to stop such behavior. Why should I attack my own love, power, or worthiness because of something said or done outside of myself?

Another way that a woman's inner Samson may turn negative is by expressing himself in a primitive unconscious drive for power. Early on, a woman in our culture is taught that to be feminine is to be weak, dependent, and helpless, not powerful. We are typically not taught to claim our legitimate feminine power. Though many reasons may be responsible for failure to claim our inner power, we typically search for it outside of ourselves. Being unaware of our inner Samson, we feel weak, helpless, and inadequate and then search for power outside of ourselves to fill this illusory belief of being powerlessness and weak. In this situation, our inner Samson typically becomes a drive for power. Outwardly such a woman may appear compliant, helpless, interested, compassionate, or helpful, but in reality, she is unconsciously consumed with a desire for power. This unconscious desire for power from our negative Samson can be seen in the Boss and Social Climbing types of women.

As the name implies, the Boss type of woman insists on getting her way. She is interested only in confirming her own opinions and dominates others who stand in her way. She is driven to always be right and is more concerned with winning an argument than trying to understand a point of view. The feminine values of forgiveness, love, and relatedness are thrown out the window in the search for external power and domination. Jezebel and her daughter, Athaliah, illustrate such domination by a negative Samson power drive.

Jezebel, who married Ahab of Israel, was so domineering that she soon became master of her husband and, in turn, the despot of a nation. One of her first acts was to remove the prophets of the Lord and replace them with priests of a materialistic and sensual cult which worshipped Baal. In another instance, Jezebel insisted on having her own way, even to the point of killing. Her husband, King Ahab, wanted a vineyard owned by Naboth. But Naboth knew the law and refused to sell it. Jezebel was incensed that her husband, the king, could not force his subject, a common man, to sell. "Dost though now govern the kingdom of Israel?" exclaimed Jezebel. And when she saw how weak her husband was in asserting himself, she declared, "I will give thee the vineyard of Naboth the Jezreelite" (1 Kings 21:7). Then Jezebel took the matter into her own hands. She wrote letters to the officials in her husband's name and sealed them with his seal. She arranged to have Naboth falsely accused of blasphemy against God and treason against the king. The bold, heartless Jezebel knew that the penalty for these crimes was death by stoning. Naboth and his sons were subsequently stoned to death, and, in the absence of heirs, possession of the vineyard reverted to the king. Confronting her husband, Jezebel declared, "Arise, take possession of the vineyard of Naboth the Jezreelite, which he refused to give thee for money: for Naboth is not alive, but dead" (1 Kings 21:15).

Though Jezebel was successful in her treacherous plot to get her way, she aroused the religious zeal of Israel's common man of whom Elijah became the aggressive leader. Elijah predicted that dogs would lick the blood of Ahab in the very field which had been acquired from Naboth and that Jezebel would be eaten by dogs. Though Elijah's predictions proved true, Jezebel's evil lived after her. Her daughter, Athaliah, carried the fatal influence from her mother into Judah when she married Jehoram. Our father's, as well as our mother's, inner men help shape the development of our own inner masculine side.

Another way in which this unconscious power aspect of a negative Samson may appear in a woman's behavior is in a driving ambition and social climbing. This type of woman is concerned with good appearances at the expense of individual feelings of people in a situation or the needs of the moment. In fact, she may give up the man she loves for the one who meets the approval of society. Her ambition clouds genuine feelings of love and relatedness toward others—the heart of the feminine principle. Rivkah Kluger suggests that Miriam of the Old Testament fell victim to her ambitious inner Samson on one occasion.

> And Miriam and Aaron spake against Moses because of the Ethiopian woman whom he married: for he married an Ethiopian woman. And they said, Hath the Lord indeed spoken only by Moses? Hath he not spoken also by us? And the Lord heard it… And the anger of the Lord was kindled against them; and he departed. And the cloud departed from off the tabernacle: and, behold, Miriam became leprous, white as snow: and Aaron looked upon Miriam, and, behold she was leprous… And Moses cried unto the Lord saying, Heal her now, O God, I beseech thee. And the Lord said unto Moses, If her father had but spit in her face, should she not be ashamed seven days? Let her be shut out from the camp seven days, and after that let her be received in again. Numbers 12:1-14

Here Miriam reveals her ambition to be as strong as Moses. Power took the place of love. In wanting to be just as great a prophet as Moses, she no longer related to him with her feeling but instead measured herself against him. Miriam was then struck with leprosy, suggesting that if she kept such an attitude she would die. However . . . "Moses asked God to deliver her, and after seven days of purification she healed and returned to the tribe" (1 Kings 12:13-15).

A contemporary example of a woman driven by her ambition and desire for power can be found in *Feminine Force* by Georgette Mosbacher. Georgette was a working-class girl who moved to California to find her fortune. She "wanted glamour . . . and power" but at first did not realized that it was inside of her. Recalling when she met George Barrie, CEO of Faberge, Georgette states:

> A new little voice inside me egged me on. Needless to say, it wasn't my inner voice. It was the seductive, rationalizing voice of ambition and immaturity. It had very little to do with who I really was. But the words it spoke made my heart race.

She thought that all she had to do was to "attach herself to him and watch her career soar." "I had foolishly sacrificed my own life in so many ways and attached myself almost exclusively to his world. I was bewitched by power. I was simply too ambitious to see that, and it took a few years of misery with G.B. (George Barrie) for me to understand it at a gut level."

In both the Boss and the Social Climber, a woman's drive for power is not tempered by the heart of her inner feminine principle and her inner Samson is serving her ego needs and desires. She is separated from forgiveness, love, and relatedness toward others by her search for the power she gave up. Rejecting the power of our inner Samson typically results in an external search for this power—a search for where it is not, thus assuring that we will not find it. And each time an external power idol that we have falls, we will feel helpless and weak.

By realizing and accepting our inner Samson, we can learn that his power lies inside of us and not out in the world. We can then direct the energy of Samson away from meeting our ego needs and combine him with the feminine values of forgiveness, love, and relatedness. In this way, our inner Samson can provide us with inner power and strength but without bossing or judging others. The crucifixion illustrates how Christ claimed His power, yet stayed connected to these feminine values. When Christ was attacked verbally and physically by the mob, He never gave up the connection with God and thus His inner Divine power. Most of us attack back when we are attacked. Because we believe that another's attack can weaken us, we behold ourselves as weakened when we are attacked. And regarding ourselves as weakened and unequal to another, we attempt to equalize the situation. We use attack to do so because we believe attack was successful in weakening us. Thus, when another person attacks us, we give up our inner power and perceive ourselves as weak and vulnerable— we attack our own inner power. We then attack the other person. But to attack another is to say that our safety and power lies in being cruel. What a funny place for it to be. When Christ was attacked at His crucifixion, He never gave up His connection with the God within from whom all power comes. If He had defended himself, He would have come from a position of weakness. No one defends himself unless he has perceived himself as weak and vulnerable. Instead, Christ stayed connected with His inner power and offered His attackers forgiveness and love. His power stayed connected with the inner feminine principle of forgiveness and love. He returned love for attack and when He transcended, He showed that even physical attack has no effects on one's true being.

In the Clinging-Vine Mother, the Judge, the Boss, and the Social Climber, we see how our inner Samson can serve our ego needs and block integration with the feminine principle and thus the true expression of our femininity. But we have also seen how he can provide us, like Esther, with inner courage, strength, and power to face the world in a feminine, not masculine, way. By balancing our inner Samson with feminine values, we can walk in wholeness in this world.

The first step in the process of redirecting our inner Samson begins with becoming consciously aware of this aspect of our personalities. Our first awareness is typically associated with his negative behaviors. We may see our own negative mothering, judging, bossing, or social climbing side. With this conscious awareness comes the freedom to choose again and redirect our inner Samson away from meeting our ego needs and demands. Georgette Mosbacher's first awareness came when her search for outer power and her ambitious drive resulted in an abusive marriage. She reported in her book that when her marriage broke up, she experienced a sense of losing power because she had projected all of her power onto G.B, her husband. Upon becoming aware of how she had looked for her power outside of herself in her relationship with her husband, Georgette says:

> . . . I was keenly aware that the life I lived wasn't going to be built by a man. What my life became was going to be entirely up to me. It was my own to create . . .

> What was becoming clearer to me was my own identity. I knew that there was absolutely no reason why, from this moment forward, the power in my life should have to be to come from a man. I was capable of creating my own identity and my own power.

My first awareness of the negative Samson in my personality was seeing him in action when I felt hurt. I found that whenever I got hurt in relationships, my inner Samson flexed his powerful muscles in a negative way. I could really feel his power welling up inside of me. This feeling was actually what I felt from my own biological father who was a strong Sampson or Tarzan type of man. Many Jungian analysts have stated that our father tempers our own inner man or animus development. During this experience, I wouldn't listen to any form of logical reasoning and became a judge condemning the other person. I then made plans of revenge to pay the other person back. When this happens now, I treat my Samson as though he were an actual inner person. I talk to him and try to comfort him just as I would with a real man who is angry. In essence, I called the inner love of my feminine side to soothe and calm my angry inner Samson—healing the negative masculine by uniting with this positive aspect of the feminine principle. I then pointed out to him that it was I who attacked myself with thoughts that resulted in my hurt feelings. The hurtful feelings were not produced in me by things occurring outside of myself; rather, I attacked my own inner power because of something another said or did. The mind that God gave each of us is so powerful that if we use it to attack ourselves, we will feel weakened and attacked. Thus, when I attacked myself, I felt weakened and I then blamed the other person for this. At this point, I verbally reclaim my inner power. I welcome back my inner Samson. I rid myself of the judging and revengeful negative Samson by applying the feminine principles of forgiveness and love. In each of these steps I am mending my inner Samson by connecting him with aspects of my inner feminine principle.

Another way that we can become aware of our inner man is to note the kind of outer man to whom we are attracted. Let me explain what I mean by examining what happens psychologically between a man and a woman when they fall in love. The woman has unconsciously projected her inner man outward onto an actual man. And her man has projected his inner woman onto her. This is what creates the basis for attraction and fascination between the sexes. It also explains the love-at-first-sight phenomenon. Romeo and Juliet provide a good example of such projections and resulting romantic love and fascination. However, in Romeo and Juliet, as well as a number of other such stories, we see a tragic ending; the lovers die. Though the typical love story in everyday life does not end in physical death, there is a type of death that occurs. The unconscious projections gradually begin to crumble, and the lover becomes a real external person instead of an idealized image. This begins to happen after a couple get married or have been around one another for a period of time. The wife or husband, in response to his or her mate's behavior in some situation, may think or say, "Why are you doing that? You're not supposed to behave that way. I didn't know you thought that way." What they are coming to realize is the difference between their own unconscious projections on each other and who they really are as persons. This dying of unconscious projections initially creates difficulties in the marital relationship, but if weathered and dealt with, it can result in a real relationship between two people, rather than a mere intertwining of idealized fantasies. Actually, a woman's outer man can help her become aware of and develop her inner man just as she can help him develop his inner woman or feminine side. In this way a man is a helpmate to a woman and a woman is a helpmate to a man. Unfortunately, some people have rejected the idea of helpmate because some Christians have traditionally associated the concept with inferiority and superiority. As a woman and man become aware of their unconscious contrasexual aspect, they become more whole as persons. Their relationship changes in that two whole people are relating to each other rather than two half people relating to create a whole.

Now let's consider again the type of outer men that we find attractive and use this as a way to become aware of our unconscious inner man. Keep in mind that these parts of ourselves, of which we are unconscious, are projected outward onto other people. This occurs not only with our inner man but also with those qualities in ourselves that we dislike but don't see. Christ points to this in Luke.

> And why beholdest thou the mote that is in thy brother's eye, but perceivest not the beam that is in thine own eye? Either how canst thou say to thy brother, Brother, let me pull out the mote that is in thine eye, when thou thyself

beholdest not the beam that is in thine own eye? Thou hypocrite, cast our first the beam out of tine own eye, and then shall thou see clearly to pull out the mote that is in thy brother's eye. Luke 6:41-42

Thus, the type of actual man that we are attracted to reflects the inner man that we are unaware of. Consider for moment the type of men that you are or have been attracted to in your life. There are many types: Tarzans, professors, football players, Tom Hanks, Ernest Hemingways, ministers, scientists, scholars, and John Wayne types of men. If you are typically attracted to the Tarzan or athletic type of man, it's highly probable that your unconscious inner man is Samson. That is, you project your strength and courage outward onto him, and hopefully he is teaching you about this aspect of your personality. If you are typically attracted to one of the other types of men listed above, you are probably unconscious of these aspects of your inner masculine side. In the following chapters, I will discuss the other aspects of our inner masculine side, both their positive and negative manifestations, and in the case of the negative expressions how to redirect them by positively balancing them with various aspects of the feminine principle.

Chapter 3

MASCULINITY TO FEMININITY: DAVID

Why do people walk on me all the time? My next door neighbor talked on the phone for two hours this morning. I didn't say anything, but I really needed to wash clothes. And the man at the garage charged me six dollars for one little fuse in my car. I knew he was overcharging me, but I decided not to say anything. I wish that I had not bought that dress this afternoon, but the salesclerk was so pushy. I look like a head of lettuce in it. I don't understand people these days; they don't respect you. It makes me so angry. They'll walk all over you.

The thing this woman doesn't understand is that she's letting herself be walked on by other people. But why do some women let themselves become door mats for others?

My life seems like an out-of-control merry-go-round. I know that I plan things out, but I always feel like I'm spinning around in a circle. Take today, for example, I planned to clean the refrigerator and the kitchen cabinets before picking the kids up after school and going grocery shopping. I was going to do this cleaning right after dropping the kids off and finishing my needle point classes this morning. It's too late now. I feel like the Mad Hatter. I don't have time to even say hello or goodbye to my children. It doesn't do any good to try and plan things. Oh well, I'd better get started on dinner. My husband is bringing his boss home to eat with us.

Should this woman's planning stop or is she planning so much that she spins like a top? Why do some women try to do so much that they feel like the Mad Hatter in *Alice in Wonderland*?

I only want to be left alone, to go my own way and live my own life. I don't set out to attract men, and I certainly do not want to estrange them from their wives and sweethearts. Why do all the women shun and mistrust me? I want to be good. But wherever I go, men follow me. They offer to take me home and even make improper advances to me. Is it my fault? I don't want it. But the poor things are so unhappy that I simply must comfort them as far as I can; only a woman with a heart of stone could do less. But I always send them home to their wives or sweethearts. Can I help it if they come back?

"What a story," we may say to ourselves! But is she telling the truth? Why do some women have the alluring qualities of a mermaid that so easily attract men to them?

What do these three different types of women, the Door Mat, the Spinning Top, and the Mermaid, have in common with one another? All three have failed to become aware and transform their inner man, David, and the true expression of their femininity is distorted. This inner man is disconnected from several aspects of the inner feminine principle and is serving the ego needs and desires of these women. As a result, this dynamic causes a negative distortion in the expression of their femininity.

I think of David in the Old Testament as symbolizing this attribute of a woman's inner man. In brief, this aspect of one's inner man, when realized and properly directed, can provide a woman with assertiveness, initiative, the capacity for planned action, and the ability to make decisions and stand by them. He also puts women in touch with her basic feelings, her drive for relatedness, and her feminine sexual instincts. Let's examine the life of David to get a feel for this aspect of our inner man.

David's capacity to be assertive and take the initiative can be seen early in his life when he defeated Goliath. Upon hearing Goliath say:

> ...choose you a man for you, and let him come down to
> me. If he be able to fight with me, and to kill me, then
> will we be your servants: but if I prevail against him, and
> kill him, then ye shall be our servants, and serve us...Let
> no man's heart fail because of him; thy servant will go and
> fight with this Philistine... And David said to Saul, let no
> man's heart fail because of him; thy servant will go and
> fight with this Philistine. I Samuel 17:8-32

Unlike the men of Israel who fled from Goliath, David took the initiative in response to his challenge. That David, a youthful shepherd boy, defeated Goliath, the personification of physical power, suggests to me that he possessed a quality different from Samson. Though both Samson and David defeated their giants with God's help, the manner in which they attained their victories was different. Samson used pure physical strength to destroy his Philistine captives; David, however, used a different strategy to combat his Philistine enemy. He refused the traditional sword and armor weapons given by Saul. Instead, he faced Goliath with a staff, "five smooth stones out of the brook," and a sling. Imagine the psychological effect this had on Goliath.

> And the Philistine said unto David, Am I a dog, that thou
> comest to me with staves? And the Philistine cursed David
> by his gods. I Samuel 17:43

David's strategy not only upset his enemy, thereby giving him a psychological advantage, but also it was smart for David to use weapons with which he was familiar and which did not require great physical strength.

David's character as a man of action in the military is clearly reflected in the following passages:

> Then answered one of the servants, Behold, I have seen a
> son of Jesse, the Bethlehemite, who is skillful in playing,
> and a mighty, valiant man, and a man of war, and prudent
> in matters, and an agreeable person, and the Lord is with
> him. I Samuel 16:18

> For, said Hushai, thou knowest thy father and his men,
> that they are mighty men, and they are chafed in their
> minds, as a bear robbed of her whelps in the field: and
> thy father is a man of war, and will not lodge with the
> people... And he also that is valiant, whose heart is as the
> heart of a lion, shall utterly melt: for all Israel knoweth
> that thy father is a mighty man, and they which be with
> him are valiant men. II Samuel 17:8-10

Time after time David went as leader of his men to conquer:

> Wherefore David arose and went, he and his men, and
> slew of the Philistines two hundred men... I Samuel 18:27

> And David and his men went up, and invaded the
> Geshurites, and the Girsites, and the Amalekites...
> I Samuel 27:8

And the king and his men went to Jerusalem unto the Jebusites, the inhabitants of the land: which spake unto David, saying, Except thou take away the blind and the lame, thou shalt not come in hither: thinking, David cannot come in hither. Nevertheless David took the strong hold of Zion: the same is the city of David. II Samuel 5:6-7

And after this it came to pass that David smote the Philistines... And he smote Moab... and so the Moabites became David's servants, and brought gifts. David smote also Hadadezer, the son of Rehob, King of Zobah, as he went to recover his border at the river Euphrates... And when the Syrians of Damascus came to succor Hadadezer, King of Zobah, David slew of the Syrians two and twenty thousand men...and the Syrians became servants to David and brought gifts. II Samuel 8:1-5

And David gathered all the people together, and went to Rabbah, and fought against it, and took it... And he brought forth the people who were therein, and put them under saws, and under harrows of iron, and with axes of iron, and made them pass through the brick kiln... thus did he unto all the cities of the children of Ammon... II Samuel 12:29-31

But David also went to save:

Then they told David, saying, Behold, the Philistines fight against Keilah, and they rob the threshing floors... So David and his men went to Keilah and fought with the Philistines, and brought away their cattle, and smote them with a great slaughter. So David saved the inhabitants of Keilah. I Samuel 23:1-5

And it came to pass, when David and his men were come to Ziklag on the third day, that the Amalekites had invaded

the south, and Ziklag, and smitten Ziklag, and burned
it with fire...And David's two wives were taken captive...
And David was greatly distressed...And David smote them
from the twilight even unto the evening of the next day...
And David recovered all that the Amalekites had carried
away; and David rescued his two wives. I Samuel 30:1-18

But when the Philistines heard that they had anointed
David King over Israel, all the Philistines came up to seek
David: ...And David... smote the Philistines from Geba
until thou come to Gazer. II Samuel 5:17-25

What a man of action, this warrior David! But David was more than a
valiant warrior; he was a skilled general. One of the reasons King Saul was
defeated by the Philistines was his poor strategy of using frontal attacks.
David, however, resorted to guerrilla tactics which eventually freed Israel
and Judah from Philistine domination.

David's initiative and capacity for planned action can also be seen in
his abilities as a diplomat and statesman. His skillful management of events
following Saul's death paved the way for his ascent to the throne of Israel.

And they mourned, and wept, and fasted until evening:
for Saul, and for Jonathan his son, and for the people of
the Lord, and for the house of Israel; because they were
fallen by the sword. II Samuel 1:12

Though David was grieved at Saul's death, he wisely and shrewdly
ingratiated himself with the elders of Israel by showing proper deference
to the memory of Saul. By political maneuvering, including gifts sent to
the elders of Judah, David was anointed king over the house of Judah.

A third event that may have been skillfully used by David to enhance his
chances of becoming Israel's king was Abner's deflection from Ish-bosheth.

And Abner sent messengers to David on his behalf, saying,
Whose is the land? Saying also, Make thy league with me,
and, behold, my hand shall be with thee, to bring about all
Israel unto thee. And he said, Well; I will make a league
with thee; that is, thou shalt not see my face, except thou
first bring Michal Saul's daughter, when thou comest to
see my face. II Samuel 3:12-13

Before he could negotiate with Abner, David insisted on and succeeded
in having Michal restored to him as his wife, for after David's flight Saul
had given her in marriage to Palti Laish. David must have believed that
this marriage into the house of Saul would make him more acceptable to
Israel. When Ish-bosheth, king of the northern tribes, met a violent end
at the hands of Recab and Baana, the path was clear for David to ascend
the throne of Israel. As King of Israel, David initiated his plan to unite all
of Israel under his rule. David's reign was spent largely in foreign wars.
When he rose to power, he was confronted by the challenge of beating
back and overcoming the attacks of lesser nations which surrounded his
country—Moab, Edom, Ammon, Aram—and thus enlarging the frontiers
of Israel. He also freed Israel and Judah from Philistine domination. Earlier
disastrous defeats by the Philistines under King Saul resulted primarily
from the iron weapons that they used. But King David shifted not only
the military but also the agricultural economy to iron. Thus, improved
weapons and skillful tactics resulted in David's defeating the Philistines.

Further evidence of David's skills and capacity for planned action
can be seen within domestic affairs. Here again, he used his abilities
to unite all of Israel. In an act of political genius, he moved to create
Jerusalem as a political and religious capital that would be beyond and
above the influence of tribal jealousies. This City of David was to symbolize
Israel as a united nation. King David then proceeded to reorganize the
administrative officials such as scribes, recorders, ministers, stewards, and
secretaries. Another advance he made was in the administration of the law.

Previously, the tribal elders acted as judges, but this function was taken over by David directly, or by judges he appointed. Having established his court at Jerusalem and centralizing the governmental agencies there, David proceeded with his plan to stabilize the religious life of his people. In the past, the unity of the Israelites had been weakened by the lack of a religious center, which could bring together these individualized tribes.

> And they brought in the ark of the Lord, and set it in its place, in the midst of the tabernacle that David had pitched for it: and David offered burnt offerings and peace offerings before the Lord. II Samuel 6:17

The City of David now became Zion, City of God, for God's presence once again dwelled in the midst of Israel. David followed this step by appointing new heads of the priesthood. Abiathar and Zadok, both of whom had a distinguished ancestry and were loyal to the king, were selected as head priests. In this way David strengthened his crown with religious traditions of the past.

A final policy that King David instituted that reveals his astuteness was the re-establishment of the Levitical cities. The religious leaders of the tribes, among whom the Levites were very influential, were often the centers of rebellion against the king. David, therefore, held it to be better for the unification of Israel to have them scattered over the country so that their power and influence could be weakened. On the positive side, their dispersal over the land would also increase the chances of bringing the God of Israel to the people.

Though David was a valiant warrior and skillful as a general, statesman, and diplomat, he was not cold and aloof emotionally. We can see his capacity for making and holding loyal friends on many occasions.

> Then Jonathan and David made a covenant, because he loved him, as his own soul. And Jonathan stripped himself of the robe that was upon him, and gave it to David, and

his garments, even to his sword, and to his bow, and to his girdle. I Samuel 18:3-4

> And the King said, Is there not yet any of the house of Saul, that I may shew the kindness of God unto him? And Ziba said unto the king, Jonathan hath yet a son, who is lame on his feet...Then King David sent, and fetched him out of the house of Machir...And David said unto him, Fear not: for I will surely shew thee kindness for Jonathan thy father's sake, and will restore thee all the land of Saul thy father; and thou shalt eat at my table continually. II Samuel 9:3-7

David paid just as much attention to small details as to larger matters. He never neglected details and remained aware of individual needs. Such behavior undoubtedly gave him an ingratiating and charming manner, which appealed to many people. Certainly, this contributed to the charisma of this leader.

> And it came to pass as they came, when David was returned from the slaughter of the Philistine, that the women came out of all cities of Israel, singing and dancing, to meet King Saul, with tabrets, with joy, and with instruments of music. And the women answered one another as they played, and said, Saul hath slain his thousands, and David his ten thousands. I Samuel 18:6-7

David's popularity, however, resulted in Saul becoming jealous of him.

> David, therefore, departed from thence, and escaped to the cave, Adullam... And everyone that was in distress, and everyone that was in debt, and everyone that was in discontented, gathered themselves unto him; and he became a captain over them: and there were with him about four hundred men. I Samuel 22:1-2

Though Saul sought to kill David, it did not stop people from submitting to his leadership. This situation with Saul also provides an example of how David acted from his feeling side. On two occasions David was in a position to kill King Saul but spared his life. David also showed deep compassion to his son Absalom, who led a rebellion against him.

> And the king commanded Joab and Abishai and Ittai, saying, Deal gently for my sake with the young man, even with Absalom. And all the people heard when the king gave all the captains charge concerning Absalom.
> II Samuel 18:5

Joab, however, killed Absalom, and David showed the depth of his feelings in losing his son.

> And the king was much moved, and sent up to the chamber over the gate, and wept: and as he went, thus he said, O my son Absalom, my son, my son Absalom! would God I had died for thee, O Absalom, my son, my son. II Samuel 18:33

A mere glance at the Psalms written by David leaves one with no doubt about the intensity of his feelings. A gamut of human emotions is expressed there. This aesthetic man not only communicated his personal feelings beautifully through poetry, but also across the strings of the harp that he played. David's emotions, however, could be kindled into a storm of passion. Upon hearing that Nabal refused to give his men provisions, David said to his men, "Gird ye every man his sword." But his anger vanished under the beauty and charm of Abigail, Nabal's wife. Beyond her beauty, Abigail's tactics were irresistible. She bowed before David and, in word as well as manner, showed deference due a sovereign. She argued her husband's cause on the ground of David's interest rather than of Nabal's. She implied that such behavior would not befit a man who was truly destined to become a monarch. Abigail also offered David a generous peace offering, which amounted to provisions for several days.

In another instance, David's passion drives him not only to commit adultery:

> And it came to pass in an eveningtide, that David arose from his bed, and walked upon the roof of the king's house: and from the roof he saw a woman washing herself; and the woman was very beautiful to look upon. And David sent and enquired about this woman. And one said, Is not this Bathsheba... And David sent messengers, and took her; and she came in unto him, and he lay with her... And the woman conceived, and sent and told David, and said, I am with child. II Samuel 11:2-5

but also to pervert his initiative and capacity for planned action into a murderous scheme:

> And David sent to Joab, saying, Send me Uriah... And David said to Uriah, Go down to thy house, and wash thy feet. and Uriah departed out of the king's house, and there followed him a mess of meat from the king. II Samuel 11:6-8

Here we see David's initial plan to remedy the situation. He orders Uriah, Bathsheba's husband, home in hopes that he would sleep with his wife and thereby think he was father to her child. David even honors Uriah by sending him gifts. However, Uriah sleeps with the servants in David's court. When asked why he did not go home:

> And Uriah said unto David, The ark, and Israel, and Judah abide in tents; and my lord Joab, and the servants of my lord, are encamped in the open fields; shall I, then go into mine house, to eat and drink, and to lie with my

wife? as thou livest, and as thy soul liveth, I will not do
this thing. II Samuel 11:11

David then initiated his final strategy that resulted in the death of
Uriah.

And it came to pass in the morning, that David wrote a
letter to Joab, and sent it by the hand of Uriah. And he
wrote in the letter, saying, Set ye Uriah in the forefront of
the hottest battle, and retire ye from him, that he may be
smitten, and die. II Samuel 11:14-15

Thus, we see in the person of David not only a man of action, but also
a man of emotion. As a man of action, David was a valiant warrior and a
skilled general, statesman, and diplomat. His initiative and capacity for
planned action united all of Israel under one rule. As a man of emotion,
David expresses the depth of his feelings through his relationships with
others, through his psalms, and through the music of his harp. However,
when David's feelings were linked with his ego needs and desires, he could
storm into passion, driving him to use his talents negatively.

Deborah of the Old Testament provides a good example of a woman
with initiative and the ability to plan and take a stand. The word Deborah
means a "bee" or "orderly motion." It's an appropriate name for this
dynamic woman who busied herself so tirelessly with the affairs of Israel
and destroyed its enemies in the Battle of Armageddon.

Deborah lived during the period of the Judges when the Israelites were
under the domination of King Sisera of Canaan. It was a time of constant
raiding, murder, and robbery. There was no unity in Israel at this time,
and the people went "a whoring after other gods."

Deborah dwelt in the south under the palm tree between Ramah
and Bethel. The people of Israel came to her for help. Now it was time for
Deborah to act and she

> ...called Barak, the son of Abinoam, out of Kedeshnaphtali, and said unto him, Hath not the Lord God of Israel commanded, saying, Go and draw toward Mount Tabor, and take with thee ten thousand men of the children of Naphtali and of the children of Zebulun? Judges 4:6

Here Deborah reminds Barak of the plan that will allow them to win and not only inspires him to put it into action but also goes with him to help carry it out. "I will surely go with thee," Deborah said, and "the Lord shall sell Sisera into the hand of a woman." Deborah, a woman chosen by the people to be a leader, defeats Sisera with her initiative and ability to stand against his nine hundred chariots of iron. Now let's look at some of the ways that our inner David, if unrecognized and improperly directed, can distort and stand in the way of our femininity being positively extended into the world.

In the Doormat type of woman, David does not perform his function of helping her to be assertive and take a stand in life. The failure of David to properly perform this function is due to many reasons, several of which will be mentioned here. Like the power aspect of our inner Samson, the culture has taught us that to be feminine is to be quietly submissive, not assertive and direct. Many of us have responded to this teaching by repressing our inner David and not allowing him to perform his proper function. The early feminist movement of the sixties and seventies encouraged women to develop the assertive aspect of David and take a stand in the world.

During my internship at a pain clinic in Dallas, Texas, I saw the results of the repression of David in a lady with rectal pain. She was a secretary and had rectal pain for ten years. She had been everywhere trying to find a way to get rid of this pain. Her personality testing revealed that she was a very dependent person who never stood up in the world, nor in her family. During our therapy session, I asked her what had been going on in her life ten years ago when the rectal pain first started. She told me that her daughter got married and she did not like her daughter's husband then and still didn't like him. About this time, I received the medical report that she had a muscle in her rectum that was in a continual state of spasm. I associated this with the marriage in the sense that this event gave her a pain in the butt. In further sessions she told me how she had let her husband's family walk on her for over twenty years. I then thought what a pain in the butt that would be. Putting this information together, I concluded that her rectal pain was due to the repression of David. Rather than take a stand in the world and express her feelings, she repressed the dislike of her son-in-law and held this feeling tightly in her rectal muscle, which caused it to spasm up and create pain in this area of her body. I related this to her, and told her that the resolution of her pain problem was to take a stand like David and express her feelings. She did not believe this for several days. Then, one night, she came for her individual session and said, "I know what you mean." She then proceeded to tell me that she had gone down to her room after the group session and saw the clothes she had asked her husband to bring to the hospital. He had gone to the back of her closet at home and had gotten clothes she was going to give to Goodwill. She said that when she saw the clothes, her rectal pain shot sky high. She realized that the muscle spasm was due to repressed feelings and in this case anger. The answer to her pain problem was to develop the assertive aspect of her David inner man and let him connect her with her feelings rather than letting them be repressed and converted into pain in the butt area of her body.

Another factor that may contribute to our inner David not performing his function properly is our attitude toward ourselves. If we view ourselves, our inner feminine being, as negative, inadequate, or somehow wrong, we may thwart David from expressing what we really think or feel. We don't allow David to express what we consider as unworthy or what we think might be perceived by others as unworthy. It is curious to me that some people will go to such lengths to repress and prevent David from performing his proper role, but never use an ounce of energy to question the original negative assumptions about themselves. For whatever reason, we hold tenaciously to the idea of our unworthiness and never question it as being unreal. In fact, it's rather arrogant to worship or have more faith in our unworthiness than in our worthiness considering what God has told us about ourselves.

> And God said, let us make man in our image, after our likeness.... So God created man in his own image, in the image of God created he him... And God saw everything that he had made; and behold, it was very good...
> Genesis 1:26-31

Here God clearly states that we are created in His image and what He created is good. To me, it seems rather arrogant to worship our unworthiness when God has clearly told us that we are worthy. True humility is to agree with God and accept His evaluation of us.

One of the main things I had to resolve to get my inner David to begin crawling toward taking a stand in the world was to deal with my concern that he might hurt another person's feelings. I was caught between a desire to be assertive and not want to be unloving and hurt another's feelings. It wasn't until I began reading the many books on assertion that appeared in the sixties and seventies that I was able to reconcile this in my mind. Here I discovered that to remain passive was to deny myself of my rights as a human being, whereas to be aggressive was to deny the other person her/his rights as a human being. Being assertive didn't mean telling the other person off, dehumanizing, or judging them. I could be assertive with love and consideration of the other person's feelings. Again, we see that the masculine component, in this case David, is balanced or complemented with the feminine principle of love. Assertion can easily turn into aggression without this balance with the heart. Some of the feminists in the sixties and seventies and today's "gender" feminists have displayed more aggression, particularly toward men and what they call the patriarchal culture, than true assertion balanced with love and respect for others.

Abigail, in the Old Testament, illustrates how a woman can take a stand yet at the same time consider the other person's feelings. Abigail, the wife of Nabal, lived when David was an outlaw in the surrounding desert. In return for protection by David and his men, the farmers paid them grain at harvest time or wool at shearing time. When David heard that Nabal was sheep-shearing, he sent ten young men to remind him that during the past season they had protected his sheep and shepherds. However, Nabal bluntly replied, 'Who is David?" This was a deliberately rude question. When David heard of it, he said, "Gird ye on every man his sword." And they set out to slay Nabal. Abigail heard of the incident and took the initiative to undo her husband's mistake. She did this not by taking an aggressive stand, but by humbling herself and appealing to David's gentler side.

> And when Abigail saw David, she hastened, and lighted from the ass, and fell before David on her face, and bowed to the ground.... I pray thee, forgive the trespass of thine handmaid... I Samuel 25:23-28

In humbling herself and owning the shadowy part of her husband's behavior, Abigail soothes David's anger. She then appeals to David's better side.

> ...for the Lord will certainly make my Lord a sure house...I Samuel 25:28

Abigail calls David to himself by reminding him that one day he would be king over Israel. We can see from her behavior how our inner assertive David can be used in conjunction with our feminine love. In this way, the heart approach of our femininity is reconciled with the assertive aspect of our inner David.

The sixties and seventies saw a surge of books on how a woman can become more assertive, which suggests to me an attempt to develop this assertive aspect of David. Some women, however, have gone to extremes with this. They have developed an assertion neurosis in which they aggressively state their opinions and feelings in every situation. Needless to say, this is done without consideration for the feelings of others. A number of things probably combined to produce this pendulum swing of David. For many years, women believed the cultural teaching that assertiveness was unfeminine and they remained passive. David has been caged within their minds undomesticated with the heart of the feminine principle. But with practice his assertive energies can be combined with the loving heart-centered feminine aspect, allowing a woman to take a more balanced stand in the world.

Another way in which our inner David can become separated from and distort our femininity can be seen in what I call the Spinning Top woman. Here David gets so involved in doing and organizing things in the world or at home that a woman doesn't take time to consider feelings. At home she may consider a clean orderly house that runs on her schedule as more important than the feelings of her family. In her book, *Revolution from Within*, Gloria Steinem talks about how she used the masculine energy of "doing" to cover her feelings.

> Like a soldier who is wounded but won't lie down for fear of dying, I just kept marching. Why? Well, if I stopped, I would have given up the way I made myself "real"—that is, by being useful to people in the outside world—just as I had made myself "real" as a child by keeping so busy that I numbed the sad unreality at home where I looked after my mother.

Marianne Williamson, in her book entitled *A Woman's Worth*, also discusses how we can become trapped in the doing energy of our masculine side.

> When we were taught as children, and most of us were,
> that our value lies in what we do as opposed to who we are,
> we automatically switched to a masculine psychological
> mode—doing, doing, doing—in order to feel worthy.

The story of Martha and Mary provides a good biblical example of women of this type.

> But Martha was cumbered about much serving, and came
> to him and said, Lord, dost thou not care that my sister
> hath left me to serve alone? bid her therefore, that she
> help me. And Jesus answered, and said unto her, Martha,
> Martha, thou art careful and troubled about many
> things. But one thing is needful, and Mary hath chosen
> that good part which shall not be taken away from her.
> Luke 10:40-42

Here we see Martha busy with her pots and pans and annoyed that Mary is enjoying herself. Martha breaks into their discussion with an indignant: "You sit there doing nothing while I'm working my fingers to the bone." Unlike Abigail, Martha's assertion includes an angry rebuke: "Lord, dost thou not care that my sister hath left me to serve alone?" But Jesus says to her, "Martha, Martha," mentioning her name twice, and thus putting real emphasis on what followed, "thou art careful and troubled about many things." Martha's inner David is not connected with her feminine heart. Working and doing are more important to her than relating to others. She is more interested in achieving goals than in connecting and being. The doing energy of her masculine principle is not connected with the being energy and loving heart of her feminine principle and thus this energy is spinning out of control. Christ pointed to the problem underlying Martha's behavior when he said, "Mary hath chosen that good part which shall not be taken away from her." The "good part", the part that God created and said was good, is what Mary connected with. This "good part" that Martha does not see or considers to be unworthy is thrown away and David is used to try to get acceptance and worthiness through action. In this way David becomes perverted in a "manic doing" way.

Whether due to unconsciousness, rejection, or negative judgment of this "good part," Martha uses her inner David to serve her ego needs and try to gain what she perceives herself as lacking. David is not used as a means to express the "good part" out into the world. Rather, he is used to gain awareness or acceptance of this inner "good part." Doing is an attempt to gain awareness, approval, and acceptance of one's inner Self or God within. A woman possessed by her inner David in this way may do things for other people to the point of her own exhaustion. She may try to achieve goals to win the love that she doesn't accept or give to herself. She tries to get people outside of herself to give her the love and acceptance that she doesn't give to herself nor accept from her inner "good part." If a woman does not check David's manic pursuit of goals, plans, and achievements, he may isolate her further from her feminine side. She then comes to value her goals, plans, and achievements over relating in a personal way and being in the world.

Another way that the lack of recognition of our inner David can distort our femininity can be seen in the Mermaid type of women. You can easily spot the Mermaid Woman from the behavior of your boyfriend or husband. As she saunters by, his head may stop and his eyes bug out in a glare. In fact, when this "all-things-to-all-men" woman moves into your neighborhood or comes to a party, all the men are immediately fascinated by her. Not only do they praise her but they also compete with each other in showing her attention. When she arrives at a party, a sea of arms stretches forth to take her coat, help her to a chair, or fetch her a drink. By the end of the evening she may have been entertained with tricks from the neighborhood magician or showered with jokes by the neighborhood court jester. I am reminded of the first scene from the movie *Gone with the Wind*, where Scarlet O'Hara was sitting on the front porch of Tara surrounded by men who were enraptured by her feminine charms. A second clue that may tip you off to the presence of a Mermaid woman is the cool aloofness that you feel toward her, which may turn into criticism and blame for the defection of your boyfriend or husband. But if you make the mistake of criticizing her to your mate, you will find, to your horror, that he will defend her. He may try to compensate for what he considers your injustice and prejudice toward her by redoubling his affections toward her. If you decide to confront this type of woman, she may respond with the story presented in the first part of this chapter. But, is the story true? Let's look at what is really going on with the Mermaid Woman.

Mermaid seems a rather appropriate label for this type of woman for several reasons. First, like a mermaid, she is very beautiful. Appearance to this woman is very important. But it takes on an importance beyond appearing attractive. She dresses for the part she plays in a particular situation. She will spend considerable time making up her face and fixing her hair just so. It's almost as though she is an artist creating a mask.

Secondly, her emotional life is like the fish tail of a mermaid which signifies the cold-blooded nature of reptiles. That is, this type of woman has no real feelings for others. Instead, any apparent feelings she shows are for a purpose, to hook a man. Her lack of real emotional involvement allows her to better control the situation. For, if she really falls in love, she is no longer able to act as an impersonal controller in the situation but is herself acted upon. This type of woman may believe that she falls in love with the various men she meets and subdues, but if she marries one of her conquests, he will soon find that her idea of love is to be pampered and waited on. Her husband may tire of such devotion to her, particularly when she continues to entice other men into her life.

The final characteristic this type of woman shares with a mermaid image is the alluring and enchanting power that she has over men. You may be thinking at this point that not only are you attractive, but you get emotionally involved with men, yet they don't flock around you. So, what's the difference? It may be just this. The Mermaid Woman simply becomes the woman a man prefers or desires. That is, at some level she is aware of the image of a woman that a man projects onto her and she simply acts this out for him. She's like an actor playing whatever role a man desires—a sweetheart, wife, mother, or whatever meets the man's needs. All of her moods, emotions, and actions reflect the man's wishes. She has no real individual personality but changes with the tide with whatever man happens to flow into her life. Thus, a man feels as though he has met his soul mate. Such a woman may strike you as mysterious, vague, ambiguous, and ambivalent. She is not unlike fluid in having few or no solid attitudes or ideas of her own. This, however, makes it easier for a man to project his inner woman onto her. She is like a mirror, or pool of water, which reflects what is projected onto it. But a man sees in her definite and detailed images, which are really his own projections. The allurement and fascination of this type of woman lies in the fact that men see in her a reflection of their own inner woman. Thus, a man will feel this woman really understands him and that his true self emerges when he is with her. He is blind to the fact that she is simply reflecting a part that he does not recognize as belonging to himself. The extent to which a man is susceptible to the charms of such a woman is related to the degree to which he is aware of his own inner woman or undeveloped feminine side. If his inner woman is especially undeveloped, he will be easily fascinated. He may throw over everything, even ruin his career for her sake. We see this happening to Samson in the Old Testament when he met Delilah.

It seems to me that Naomi Wolf, in her book entitled *The Beauty Myth*, is trying to deal with some of the issues revolving around the Mermaid type of woman: the emphasis on beauty and the projections of men. Wolf explains the emphasis on physical appearance or the beauty myth which pressures women to exercise, diet, and wear make-up, is a way the patriarchal culture continues to control women. She states, "The beauty myth is not about women at all ... It's about men's institutions and institutional power."

As Dr. Sommers so aptly points out, "Much of the support Wolf brings for her beauty myth theory consists of merely labeling an activity insidious rather than showing it to be so." Wolf fails to see that in the case of Mermaid Women beauty is used to hook and control men. In terms of men's projections onto women, Wolf sees them only in terms of what men want women to be like and as a way to control women. I agree that men have projected their notions of femininity onto women; however, we have chosen to receive these projections and identify with them. In the case of the Mermaid Woman, either consciously or unconsciously, she becomes a man's projection of femininity, specifically she becomes his inner feminine side. For Wolf, the resolution to the problem of men's projections and the beauty myth lies in "an electric resurgence of the women-centered political activism of the seventies—a feminist third wave—updated to take on the new issues of the nineties." A more direct and fruitful approach to me would be to center the problem within and work on one's inner David.

Now that we have a general picture of the Mermaid Woman, let's return to the story by Esther Harding presented at the beginning of this chapter. Is the Mermaid Woman telling the truth in what she is saying? According to Esther Harding in her book *The Way of All Women*, the answer to this question is both yes and no. Esther Harding does an excellent job in pointing out the several species of Mermaid Women. She has found that some of these women are unaware of their power over men, whereas others are aware and use such power for their own ego needs and satisfaction. Thus, some Mermaid Women are telling us the truth as far as they are conscious of what's going on. But whether they are aware or unaware, the motive remains the same—to hook and hold a man. The following words from an old song adequately describe this motive— "Whatever Lola want, Lola gets, and little man little Lola wants you."

According to the work of Esther Harding, the feminine instincts in the Mermaid Woman operate unchecked in response to men. What we see here is pure natural feminine instinct seeking satisfaction of the biological sex urge. Every woman has such pure feminine instincts but usually places some restraint on them based on cultural or religious teachings. Esther Harding suggests that this type of woman comes in three sub-species. There is the flower girl who is sweet, innocent maiden-like lady who is typically, fair and pretty. Such a woman is doomed to be a child throughout her life and may have considerable trouble facing old age. She is soft and yielding and seems full of love. She directs her life toward her man. However, if one particular man is not available, another will do just as well. Her education consists primarily of how to dress and hold her tongue, though she may be deficient here. She may show a tendency to seek the center of the stage underneath her innocent maiden-like mask.

The "tiger woman" is markedly different from the "flower girl." She is passion personified and lives exactly as she feels without any calculations as to the effects of her behavior. Her boyfriend or husband never knows whether he will be greeted by her with passionate embraces, a storm of anger, or a jealous rage. She always feels strongly and her turbulent moods lure and hold some men. But why should such emotional outbursts be appealing to a man? Complete abandonment to her emotions releases in him his overly restrained or undeveloped feelings. Thus, a man can experience through her his own emotions, which are kept under thumb by rationality.

A third type of Mermaid Woman falling in this category is the "iceberg lady" who is cool, aloof, and distant to her man. She is completely passive and indifferent and expresses no wish of her own. More than likely, she is unaware of her feelings and wishes. She spends most of her time in a semi-conscious state not fully aware of what is going on around her. This may serve to protect her from reality and its requirements to make definite decisions and stand on them. She also shows an ambiguous nature—she will and she won't, again, reflecting her inability to take a definite stand. Rather than rouse herself to definite action, she will endure a marriage which is distasteful to her.

Women falling in the second general category of Mermaid Women still become what their man projects on them, but they are aware of their power over men. They may use their skills to their own advantage—to maintain a good appearance socially, to inflate their own egos, to get money, or to run a house. Most people are familiar with the first type of woman falling in this category —the Gold Digger. This feminine stockbroker's eyes ring up dollar signs whenever a man of prestige, social status, or money appears. Delilah of the Old Testament is a good example of the gold-digging Mermaid type of woman.

> And the lords of the Philistines came up onto her, and said unto her, Entice him, and see wherein his great strength lieth, and by what means we may prevail against him, that we may bind him to afflict him; and we will give thee every one of us eleven hundred pieces of silver. Judges 16:5

And on three different occasions Delilah tried to get Samson to reveal the source of his strength.

> And she said unto him, How canst thou say, I love thee, when thine heart is not with me? Thou hast mocked me these three times, and hast not told me wherein thy great strength lieth. And it came to pass, when she pressed him daily with her words, and urged him, so that his soul was vexed unto death, That he told her all his heart and said unto her, There hath not come a razor upon mine head; for I have been a Nazarite unto God from my mother's womb: if I be shaven, then my strength will go from me, and I shall become weak, and be like any other man. And when Delilah saw that he had told her all his heart, she sent and called for the lords of the Philistines, saying, Come up this

once, for he hath shown me all his heart. Then the lord of
the Philistines came up unto her, and brought money in
their hand. Judges 16:15-18

Thus, Samson was captured by the Philistines through the feminine
charms of Delilah. Though he displayed greater physical strength, he
seemed to have a weakness for feminine seduction.

Another type of woman in this category is the "Wise Wife" who uses
her charm to further a personal relationship. If she is married, she develops
skill in managing her husband and the situation between them. She uses
David's capacity for planned action to get him to meet her perceived ego
needs. She is always on hand and always anticipates her husband's wishes.
She makes home so pleasant that he, of necessity, has to fall in with her
plans and do what is expected of him. Her ends are directed toward
making her husband happy and her marriage a success. The problem here
is emphasis on the possessive pronoun—it's her husband and her marriage.
She gives only as much of her feeling as is good for him and by skillful
management of rewards keeps him in line. Her husband may come to see
behind her mask of the good wife and into her egocentric attitude.

In the various types of Mermaid Women that we have discussed, David
is not connected to the inner feminine principle and doesn't perform his
function of relating feelings into consciousness or the feminine principle
out into the world of relationships. Instead of identifying and relating
their inner feelings, these women become the feelings a man projects
onto them. They experience their femininity externally through whatever
a man projects onto them, not internally from the core of who they are.
Untempered by the feminine principle, David becomes perverted in
relationships. He schemes and maneuvers others into meeting egocentric
needs rather than performing his function of relating and connecting to
others in a meaningful, loving relationship. For the unaware Mermaid
Woman, the flower girl, the tiger lady, and the iceberg lady, David could
express their own feelings and their own feminine sexuality. David could

help them take the initiative to change their marriage and present their real feelings to their husbands. Thus, the husband could begin to discriminate her from his own projections onto her. Some of these women may not want to give up the advantages gained by carrying their mate's projected inner woman.

In the aware Mermaid Women, the Gold Digger and the Wise Wife, David is projected onto an external man who is then expected to meet all of their needs, pamper them, and show complete devotion. However, if these women were to accept their inner David, he would provide them with the capacity to act and meet their own needs. In the Gold Digger woman, David is caught in trying to satisfy such ego motives as gaining money, prestige, and status. Acceptance and redirection of David in this situation may result in using his powers in more constructive ways.

Ann Ulanov talks about two more types of women, the Shirley Temple and the Father's Daughter, who also show a problem with their inner David. The Shirley Temple type is frightened by the appearance of her inner David and is unable to go beyond seeing him as an overwhelming invader. She sees David as Goliath rather than as an inner man who will help her stand up to the Goliaths in her life. Hence, she remains the little girl that she was when he first made his appearance in her mental life.

The Father's Daughter has failed to make her inner David her own. She continues to see him only externally in her father. Thus, she remains emotionally attached to her father. This woman may send seductive signals to men of which she is unaware. But still being emotionally attached to her father, she will reject men who try to relate to her. If this type of woman gets married, she may overemphasize the individual personal relationship. She may tempt her husband away from collective responsibilities and realistic adaptation. She may overemphasize her personal relation to a man to the point of neglecting his need to establish his career, make a living, and find himself in society. This woman holds on to her man to the degree that he is unable to develop himself. She expects all of his behavior to be directed to her. She may even affect her children with this overemphasis on the individual relationship by becoming a personal friend to them, and thereby binding them to her. Just as David forgot his responsibility to God, his people, and Israel under his passion toward Bathsheba, so to our inner David, if not realized and re-directed, will cause a woman to make similar demands on her man and children. Alternatively, David may result in this type of woman becoming so concerned with the fluctuation of individual feelings that she is unable to make any permanent commitment to her own attitudes or actual relationship but spends her life in emotional wanderings and tentative attachments. Here rejection of David prevents a woman from taking a definite stand in terms of attitudes or relationships. Unlike David, who took the initiative with Goliath, who took a stand against the Philistines, and who stood firm in his desire to unite Israel, this type of woman doesn't take a definite stand and falls into tentative attachments. Some women may date a man for years and still be unable to make a definite commitment and stand by it. Her behavior reflects a "she will and she won't" attitude.

In each of the women discussed in this chapter—the Door Mat, Spinning Top, Mermaid, Shirley Temple and the Father's Daughter—we see how David can fail to perform his proper function. But if we become aware of this masculine aspect of ourselves, disconnect it from serving our ego needs and desires, and integrate it with our inner feminine principle, David can perform positively for us. He can provide us with the capacity for planned action, the ability to make decisions, relate in a very personal and emotional way to others, and take a definite stand in a feminine, not masculine, way.

Chapter 4
MASCULINITY TO FEMININITY: PAUL

I find parties a complete bore. The conversation of the female gender consists of either pots and pans or feminine emotional moonings. I prefer more lofty intellectual topics which deal with such philosophical questions as What is reality? or What are the valid ways of thinking? Why do women waste so much time with trivial personal issues?

*W*e can answer Scholarly Woman's statements with a question: Why is she flying above the personal with her lofty intellectual ideation?

Where's that man I married now? Well, it doesn't take a Sherlock Holmes to know if he's been around. I need only look in the den. Yes, he's been here. There's the flowerbed of glasses he usually plants on the T.V. tray and the fertilizing crumbs he scatters across the carpet to help it grow, I guess. He may have worked in the yard today. That man has the thumb color of a red beet. I'll check the bathroom. If the bottom of the tub looks like Astroturf, I'll know he finally mowed the grass. What a Prince Charming I married. The only thing that he rides is an old white Mustang and he never wants to be around me anymore!

Why is this woman's hero now a villain? What man wants to be ensnared and emasculated by a Nagging Wife?

> I believe a husband is the head of the household, and to be a good wife I must submit to him at all times; I must totally cater to his needs and wants. My role is to be a helpmate to my husband. I enjoy following the feminine way – being mother, cook and bedmate.

Is this truly the feminine way? Is this Patriarchal Woman really actualizing her femininity in the role of good wife or is she choosing to be the patriarchal daughter and mother to her father husband?

Here we see three different types of women on the surface—Scholarly Woman, Nagging Wife, and Patriarchal Woman—but underneath they share a similar problem. All three have failed to become aware and direct their inner man, Paul, in a balanced relationship with their feminine side. Instead, this inner man is serving their ego needs and desires. Thus, their inner Paul has become negative and distorts the true expression of their femininity. I think of St. Paul in the New Testament as symbolizing this aspect of our inner man. He can be thought of as the "bearer of the word," or an inner reasoning attitude that sees things from a more general and logical perspective. Paul represents the capacity for rational discrimination and the ability to function from an inner, rather than from the outer collective authority of the mass mind.

Paul was a Benjamite, born in Tarsus of Cilicia, to a well-to-do family. He was a man of letters who studied under Gamliel, the foremost Rabbi of his time. Paul was a Pharisee and determined to rid the Jewish community of what was called the Christian heresy. He was well versed in the letter of the law but did not have the spirit or heart of the law associated with the feminine principle. He had lost his connection to the heart of the law and was steeped in the arrogance of his ego. When we first encounter Paul in the New Testament, he is caught in the collective religious traditions of his Jewish faith and persecuting the Christians.

> As for Saul, he made havock of the church, entering into every house, and haling men and women, committed them to prison. Acts 8:3

> And Saul, yet breathing out threatenings and slaughter against the disciples of the Lord, went unto the high priest, and desired of him letters to Damascus to the synagogues, that if he found any of this way, whether they were men or women, he might bring them bound into Jerusalem. Acts 9:1-2

So, armed with authority by the chief priest, Paul started for the city of Damascus, intending to stamp out the Christian infection there. "And as he journeyed, he came near Damascus and suddenly there shone around about him a light from heaven," which left him blinded for a while but caused him to see the truth and thus freed him from the traditions of his Jewish religion. He became the bearer of the word unto many nations and claimed that God had committed to him the mission of taking Christ's teachings to the Gentiles. He and Barnabas set out to evangelize the Gentiles while Peter and the other disciples were focusing on a similar mission to the Jews. The Book of Acts narrates three different "missionary journeys" that took Paul into many cities and through incredible adventures. He taught the new converts and helped them organize for their new life in Christ and stayed as long as he felt he could and then moved on to other places.

The Epistles that Paul wrote following the Damascus experience reveal the type of man that he became. Here we see a man of great intellect and training who put forth the doctrine of the Christian church in his letters to seven of the early churches. Using his talent for rational discrimination and order, St. Paul helped develop the organization and administration of these local churches. He also clearly expounded the nature and purpose of the law; the grounds and means of the believer's justification, sanctification, and glorification; and the position, conduct, expectation, and service of the believer.

Thus, with Paul, we see a man of great intellect and rationality organized the early church and delineated the beliefs of the Christian faith. So, too, within each woman is a Paul. This inner Paul aspect of the masculine principle can provide a woman with rational discrimination and the capacity to function from an inner rather than outer collective authority. He can help give rational form, the word, to her creativity and deepest intuitions. Many women have very profound insights, but when questioned, particularly by the analytical thinking of men, they are unable to give their intuition and feelings words. This can be frustrating for women because they are certain of what they know, yet they can't fully communicate it. Men may quickly discount these feminine intuitions as nonsense because they cannot be given form in terms of the words or male rational scientific thinking associated with the use of inductive and deductive logic. The New Testament characters of Priscilla and Lydia provide good examples of women who used their inner Paul dynamic to develop the early Christian church.

Priscilla, or Prisca, was one of the most influential women in the early church. She was a Jew who had left Italy with her husband, Aquila, to live first at Corinth then about 18 months later, at Ephesus. They left Rome because Claudius expelled all Jews. That Priscilla used her inner Paul is evidenced by many facts. Priscilla and her husband were tentmakers, and their homes, in both Corinth and Ephesus, became rendezvouses for those wanting to know more about the new faith of Christianity. She became the bearer of the word. In Romans 16:3, Paul calls "Priscilla and Aquila my helpers in Christ Jesus and in I Corinthians 16:19 reported that they had a church in their home.

Saint Paul stayed with Priscilla and Aquila, and when he departed from Corinth for Syria, they went with him. They went to Ephesus, and he left them there. He committed the work in Ephesus to Priscilla and Aquilla. When he returned a year or more later, he found they had established a well-organized congregation in Ephesus. There Priscilla and Aquila ranked next to Paul and Timothy in the work of the congregation.

Not only was Priscilla a woman of scholarly attainments, she managed her household, worked as a tentmaker, and was noted for her hospitality. She didn't let her inner Paul take her away to an intellectual ivory tower; rather, she used her gifts of rationality and consciousness together with her feminine pursuits. She managed her household and kept it warmly open to others.

Lydia also shows an acceptance of her inner Paul and integration of him with her feminine side. She was a business woman, a "seller of purple," and probably one of the most successful and influential women of Philippi. She used the reasoning and discriminating aspects of her inner Paul within the business world and became the bearer of the word in Philippi. In her home was cradled the church of Philippi, whose members were later referred to by St. Paul as his "joy and crown." She was a seeker after the truth and became Europe's first convert. Though in her era she no doubt represented the new woman, a business woman who had succeeded, Lydia was generous and had a personal charm that drew people to her. She and a small group of worshippers met on the riverbank at Philippi. St. Paul and Silas went there and spoke to these women. They listened to St. Paul as he related his story of the new gospel. Soon after this encounter she was baptized, and then her whole household was baptized. She picked up the torch from St. Paul and became the bearer of the Word. She was one of many to spread the gospel of Christ through Europe.

In spreading the Word, both Priscilla and Lydia stand as real heroines against the collective religious thinking of their times. Their inner Paul provided them with an intellect, an inner reasoning quality capable of discerning the truth and communicating it to the world through the spoken word. However, both of these women retained their feminine qualities. They weren't aloof eggheads but remained caring and helpful toward others by combining these feminine attributes with their inner Paul aspect. Now let's look at some of the ways our inner Paul, if unrecognized and connected with our ego needs and demands, can negatively distort the expression of our femininity in the world.

In the Scholarly Woman, identification with Paul's rational, intellectual nature separates her from the personal subjective and warm-heartedness of the feminine side of her being. She is unconsciously possessed by her inner Paul and views life from a totally objective and logical perspective. In some cases, such a woman uses her inner intellectual Paul as a defense against experiencing her feelings. Somewhere along the road of life such a woman got deeply hurt or decided certain needs would not be met, and she identified with her inner Paul as an intellectual defender and protector.

I recall working with a lady during the mid-1970s who used her inner Paul in this way. She had fallen at work and injured the thoracic region of her back. However, when the physical injury healed, she continued to complain of pain in this area. She said that everything in life was a chore and she had to force herself to do things. Because of her discomfort, she could not drive a car very far, go to work, or do many things she used to do prior to the injury. She had literally become an invalid in her early forties. During therapy with her, I began to notice that she put a premium on being independent and was trying to find an either/or logical solution to her problems. Whenever I tried to get her to feel an emotion, she would fence with me intellectually. She was using her intellectual Paul to protect her little girl side. This "little girl" standing behind her inner Paul wanted to be dependent, loved, and protected; however, she could not consciously accept this part of herself, so it got converted into back pain. In this way she got the needs of the little girl for love and protection met by becoming an invalid. The day I confronted her with all of this she again responded intellectually without expressing any real feelings. She said, "I don't agree, but you are entitled to your opinion." I asked her what she was feeling, and she said again. "Everyone has the right to have their own opinion." I then told her that most people would feel hurt, anger, or something, when confronted with their defenses, but she would not respond with any emotion.

During the 1970s many women began going to college or professional school to develop their inner Paul and there was a temptation to abandon the personal, subjective world of the feminine. I was in graduate school during this time and recalled when I had unconsciously identified with my intellectual, rational inner Paul. I was at a July Fourth party and instead of having fun I was discussing statistics with a man at the party. A friend of mine then quietly told me that the party wasn't a seminar. As I pondered her remarks, I realized that I had forgotten how to just have a good time at a party. It wasn't until I had a dream that I finally recovered my fun-loving side again. In this dream, I was in a mall with a number of specialty shops. I walked into one of these shops and saw a little monkey. I put out my finger and the little monkey got on it so I took the monkey home with me. This dream suggests that I had re-integrated my monkey or fun-loving side, which I had repressed during my graduate training years. About a month later, I noticed that I was again able to just have fun at parties instead of participating in lofty intellectual subjects.

Another example of how professional training can separate us from our feminine side can be seen in the imagery of one of my patients at the pain clinic where I did my internship. This lady came to the clinic with back pain and mysterious swelling in her right foot. While doing a guided imagery exercise to find the meaning behind her discomfort, she got an image of the sun and a black cat. When she saw these two images during the exercise, they were split from each other by a vertical line. When we examined these two images and how they were split off from each other, they showed that her feelings, or feminine side, were split off from her intellect. She was a very intellectual woman and had been professionally trained as an engineer.

Like Priscilla and Lydia, we must hold on to our hearts and the personal aspects of the feminine principle. We must use the light of Paul to bring the feminine in balance with the masculine—not stamp it out of ourselves, our culture, or our world where it is so sorely needed.

In the Patriarchal Woman, we see Paul echoing the collective traditions that men are men and women are women and their relationship is one in which women are secondary and submissive to men. In fact, St. Paul's writings are used to confirm this type of relationship between a man and a woman. Let's look at what this type of belief means in terms of psychological development and what problems may arise from following it.

The dictum that a man can only be a man and a woman a woman forces a man to repress his inner feminine side and a woman to repress her inner masculine side. Thus, a woman is told to reject the strength, initiative, and light that her inner man can provide. But we live in a patriarchal culture that emphasizes the masculine values of initiative, consciousness, and rationality and sees feminine values of being, letting nature take its course, and intuitive thinking as inferior. This may cause a woman to consider the objective, rational masculine approach as superior in all situations and thus fail to combine it with her subjective personal feminine approach and extend it into the culture.

Also, as we have seen in previous chapters, if a woman ignores her inner man, she may fall victim to his tyranny. In turn, she may tyrannize the man in her life upon whom she has projected this tyrannous inner man. Thus, we get the Nagging Wife. She withholds her warm feelings and forgiving spirit. She will nag her husband and even berate him for not being a man. She harps on her man's weak points and sees herself as the superior of the two. In response to such put-downs, a man, in desperation to assert himself and shut the woman up, may react to her violently. I've known two such women in my life, and it's a mystery to me why their husbands put up with such berating.

I visited one of these Nagging Wife types who had just moved to a large northeastern city. That night I was talking with her husband about politics. When he left for bed at nine o'clock, she told me that she had taught him everything that he knew about politics. This started an hour-long discussion of his faults and problems. She ended her discussion with a complaint about how much time he spent away from her. He left the house at six in the morning, returned at seven in the evening, and went to bed at nine o'clock in a separate bedroom. Any free time on the weekends, he spent playing tennis. She was also upset that over the years of their married life he had to move to a new job in a different part of the country each time she joined him at his present location. The last I heard he was on the West Coast and she was alone, but still married to him, living on the East Coast.

The patriarchal form of marriage may result in another form of the nagging wife type. Here the wife becomes bitterly disillusioned with her Prince Charming who fails to be the promised hero. The husband does not relate to her personally, and she may harp endlessly on his failures. She isolates instead of uniting and uses power instead of love. Some women prevent or resolve the Nagging Wife syndrome by forcing themselves into the role of the Good Wife. They become faithful to traditional standards which actually hinder their own development. Such women consent to being confined to the narrowest definition of mother, bedmate, and cook. The Eve Reborn movement of the 1970s reflected a holding on to the traditional patriarchal views of men and women and their relationships. Even the name symbolizes a return to Eve, a symbol of the natural mother. In her 1973 book, *Total Woman*, Marabel Morgan regresses to the Good Wife role as defined by traditional patriarchal views. She begins with a romantic notion of a hero mate or Prince Charming:

> I believed in the All-American Cinderella story; marriage was roughly curtains at the kitchen window, strawberries for breakfast and loving all the time.

But then her promised hero fails to relate to her:

> I thought back to our engagement period. How romantic Charlie had been! He was such a fabulous kisser, but now there were very few kisses. Where was my passionate lover? After a few short years of married life, I found myself sighing as we sat in front of the television set. As the hero on the tube took the heroine in his arms, I yearned for Charlie to take me in his. I wanted him to smother me with kisses, to make my heart pound again in his embraces.

From her Marabel Morgan became the Nagging Wife:

> I had nagged for a new one for years and for years he had refused.

> Finally, I nagged and insisted so much that Charlie, in desperation, announced, "Look, I love the family room exactly the way it is."

> For six years I nagged Charlie on the same subjects day after day.

But Mrs. Morgan resolves her marital conflict by switching to the Patriarchal Woman:

> The biblical remedy for marital conflict is stated, "You wives submit to your husband's leadership in the same way you submit to the Lord." God planned for a woman to be under her husband's rule.

> What if the king makes the wrong decision? Oh, that's a hard one, especially when you know you're right, and there are times when that is the case. The queen is still to

91

follow him forthwith. A queen shall not nag or buck her king's decision after it is decreed.

A total woman is not a slave. She graciously chooses to adapt to her husband's way, even though at times she desperately may not want to. He in turn will gratefully respond by trying to make it up to her and grant her desires. He may even want to spoil her with goodies.

Adapting to his activities, his friends, and his food is not always easy, but it's right. I know that now. And I know when I don't want to adapt, it's my problem, not his...

Sometimes it takes a while to talk myself into adapting, but the benefits are so great. Much more important than presents are those times of tenderness. Last week Charlie took my face in his hands and planted gentle kisses all over it, the way I do to our baby's face.

Though Mrs. Morgan feels that she has gained love, she has lost something very important. She has lost herself. As Dr. Ann Ulanov puts it:

Negatively, she may lose the momentum of her own development by confining herself to the feminine role of the masculine-feminine polarity, not ever going beyond the patriarchal definition of the feminine role.

Thus, rather than letting Paul provide an inner authority and an inner reasoning attitude, some women lose themselves in the role of a good wife as defined by the mass mind.

Since Paul's writings has been used to justify this position, let's use the light of our inner Paul to examine his statements on this issue.

Wives submit yourselves unto your own husbands, as unto the Lord. For the husband is the head of the wife, even as Christ is the head of the Church: and he is the savior of the body. Therefore, as the church is subject unto Christ, so let the wives be to their own husbands in everything. Husbands, love your wives, even as Christ also loved the Church, and gave himself for it: That he might sanctify and cleanse it with the washing of water by the word, that he might present it to himself a glorious church, not having spot, nor wrinkle, or any such thing; but that it should be holy and without blemish. So ought men to love their wives as their own bodies. He that loveth his wife loveth himself. For no man ever yet hated his own flesh; but nourisheth and cherisheth it, even as the Lord the church; For we are members of his body, his flesh, and of his bones. For this cause shall a man leave his father and mother, and shall be joined unto his wife, and they two shall be one flesh. Ephesians 5:22-31

But I would have you know, that the head of every man is Christ; and the head of every woman is the man; and the head of Christ is God. I Corinthians 11:3

These biblical passages have been traditionally interpreted as saying that a wife is secondary and inferior to her husband and that she is to be under the domination of her husband. However, these passages could be pointing to a unity rather than a ladder of authority between a man and a woman. Is God above Christ in the chain of command?

...I said, I go unto the Father: for my Father is greater than I. John 14:28

This passage suggests that God is above Christ, but others point to their oneness.

Jesus saith unto him, Have I been such a long time with you, and yet hast thou not known me, Philip? he that hath seen me hath seen the Father; and how safest thou then, Shew us the Father? John 14:9

My Father, who gave them to me, is greater than all and no man is able to pluck them out of my Father's hand. I and the Father are one. John 10:29-30

But if I do, though ye believe not me, believe the works: that ye may know, and believe, that the Father is in me and I in him. John 10:38

Could it be that Christ both submits and rules? Even though He submits and rules, Jesus and God are considered to be of one substance. But doesn't Christ's relationship to the church also involve submitting and ruling. Ephesians 5:23 states that, "Christ is the head of the church; and he is savior of the body." Christ loved the church and gave Himself up for her, that He might sanctify her. In several places a man is called to respond to his wife as Christ does to the church. Does this mean that a man both rules and submits just as a woman is called to do? As Christ is one with God, so the husband is one flesh with his wife. In recent years this inferior, submissive helpmate role of woman has been questioned by a number of biblical scholars. The line in question is in Genesis 2:18 when God says, "It is not good that the man should be alone; I will make him a helper fit for him." The two key Hebrew words are "ezer kenegdo" translated "fitting helper" in the new Bible of the Jewish Publication Society, a helpmate in the Jerusalem Bible, and an aide fit for him in the Anchor Bible. But David Freedman, who studied Assyriology and northwest Semitic languages at Columbia University, said the customary translations do not convey the real meaning. He said, "woman was not intended to be merely man's helper; she was to be instead, his partner. The Hebrew word "ezer" occurs 21 times in the Hebrew Bible. Eight times the word means "savior" and the other times it means strength. David Freedman, said "when it means strength it is sometimes paralleled with the concept of majesty, as in Psalms

68:34—"Ascribe strength to God; his majesty is upon Israel, and his strength is in the heavens." The other Hebrew word, "Kenegdo", has given translators problems because it appears in the Bible only once. However, David Freedman pointed out in late rabbinical commentaries the word means "equal", as in the saying, "The study of Torah is equal to all the other commandments." In Freedman's view, there is no basis for translating "kenegdo" as fit or appropriate." Indeed, the New King James Version, a revised work by conservative scholars, uses the word comparable— "I will make him a helper comparable to him." Freedman said that if God was thought of as equal in power to Adam in Genesis 2:18, then that would match the other Genesis account of Adam and Eve's creation in Chapter 1 of this book. He stated that the biblical line "male and female he created them" does not lead one to conclude the superiority of either. Could all of this be pointing to the fact that a man and woman complement each other? A woman is a helpmate to a man, but a man is also a helpmate to a woman. But let's examine what is meant by complement and helpmate.

As stated in Chapter 2, when a woman and man fall in love with each other, there is an unconscious projection of their contrasexual nature outwardly onto their partner. That is, the woman has unconsciously projected her inner man onto an actual man. And her outer man has projected his inner woman onto her. This creates the basis for attraction and fascination between the sexes. Both consciously and unconsciously we have male and female bound together. At this stage of the relationship the woman is not aware of her own inner man; rather, she projects and sees him in her mate. The helpmate part of this relationship comes in the form of her external man helping her become aware of her own inner masculine side. He teaches her the masculine principle, shows her how she has such qualities as strength, initiative, rationality, and an inner authority. Similarly, a woman helps her mate become aware of his inner feminine qualities that he repressed in favor of conscious identification with the masculine principle. As a result of this, we then have two whole people relating to each other rather than two half people in mutual projections and dependent fascination. Thus, through the role of helpmate the complementary male-female relationship can be changed into a wholistic relationship for both a man and a woman. Two whole people are now relating to produce a super whole. From this perspective, it seems obvious why the traditional view of marriage means self-loss. Both a man and a woman are prevented from achieving wholeness and are forced into a dependent existence of mutual projections.

I observed this in a sixty-five-year-old lady whose husband died. She came into therapy to deal with her loss. As we moved through the sessions, I began to realize that her main problem stemmed from a lack of integration into awareness of her own inner masculine side. Though she was married most of her life, she had not introjected the strength, assertion, or rationality that her husband showed. She had not learned from him that these qualities were also within her. She had not let him be a helpmate to her to develop these qualities. Thus, at his death she felt at a complete loss. She had lost touch with the inner masculine aspect of her being that she had projected onto her husband and therefore felt frightened, unable to do things, and did not know how to think through things rationally.

I also saw another variety of this while working at a shelter for battered women. I couldn't understand why these women would go back to men who beat them up physically as well as mentally and emotionally. But when I began talking to these women, I discovered why. Not only did they project their inner strength and power outward onto their husbands, they projected their ability to think and reason, their inner Paul, onto them. So even though their husbands physically battered them, they returned because this was the only way they could feel protected and rationally discriminate in various situations. Without the connection with their husbands, they felt powerless, frightened, and had trouble using their rational minds.

In the Scholarly Woman, Paul's power of rational discrimination is well developed, but he is disconnected from the heart aspect of her inner feminine principle. Such a woman may be unconsciously possessed or ruled by her intellect or she may be using it to defend against her inner feelings. In her run for the presidency, Hilary Clinton showed a well-developed intellectual side but evidenced difficulty in relating to others with the emotions of an open heart. Regardless of the reason, the Scholarly Woman needs to integrate and connect her inner Paul with the heart felt emotions of her feminine principle. The intellectual power of Paul can be expanded considerably when a woman has an open and loving heart.

Acceptance of our inner Paul can also provide us with rational discrimination and the capacity to function from an inner rational rather than outer collective authority. In the Patriarchal Woman and the Good Wife, Paul is not functioning properly. Hence, these women have defined their femininity and selves in terms of collective traditions rather than from their inner being. Paul's qualities have not been integrated into consciousness, nor have they been connected with various aspects of their inner feminine principle.

The feminist movement of the sixties and seventies was the "bearer of the word" shining intellectual light on how women in their roles as Patriarchal and Good Wife types were identified with the collective cultural definitions of femininity. This was an important and necessary light because conscious awareness is the first step to change. But today some feminists continue to attack the patriarchal culture and its traditions as the source of all the problems that a woman has rather than trying to understand what is going on psychologically within herself. These feminists have been called "gender" feminists by Dr. Christina Sommers and examples of them can be found in the writings of Gloria Steinem and Naomi Wolf.

In her book, *Revolution From Within*, Gloria Steinem states, "each of us is born with a full circle of human qualities ... societies ask us to play totalitarian gender roles that divide labor, assign behavior, provide the paradigm for race and class and are so accepted that they may be seen as part of nature." In *The Beauty Myth*, Naomi Wolf says that the beauty myth "is seeking right now to undo psychologically and covertly all the good things that feminism did for women, materially and overtly." She further points out that "it (beauty myth) has grown stronger to take over the work of social coercion that myths about motherhood, domesticity, chastity and passivity, no longer can manage."

Dr Sommers, in her book *Who Stole Feminism*, maintains these second wave "gender" feminists are "preoccupied with their own sense of hurt and their own feelings of embattlement and siege." They are very different from the "first wave mainstream or equity feminists" who wanted "fair treatment without discrimination." Dr. Sommers questions the theories of these gender theorists. She believes "that how these feminist theorists regard American society is more a matter of temperament than a matter of insight into social reality." The support that Wolf brings for her beauty myth theory consists of "merely labeling an activity insidious rather than showing it to be so." Dr. Sommers also questions Faludi's Backlash Theory that men are in a conspiracy to keep women from enjoying the freedoms they earned during the seventies and eighties. She concludes that, although Faludi and Wolf "have appropriated masses of statistical data showing backlash and the beauty myth are at work in American society", real evidence is "terribly short" in supply.

Gloria Steinem, Naomi Wolf, and Susan Faludi remind me of the Nagging Wife type of women who have projected their negative inner Paul onto the culture instead of their husbands. They constantly nag and berate men in the culture as being responsible for all of their perceived problems. To attack a projection of one's inner Paul will not permanently liberate you from his tyranny, rather it will only provide temporary release from his negative effects. One has to reel in the projection and realize that the negative cultural conditioning is inside your own mind. There and only there can you deal with and let go of the negative, collective Paul type of thinking. Then one's inner Paul can function from an inner rational rather than outer collective authority. One can easily see the effects of negative Paul thinking in the writings of "gender" feminists as compared with the more objective rational approach of Dr. Sommers in her book.

These "gender" feminists proceed as if they are the sole "bearers of the word" for women in our culture. Steinem, Wolf, and Faludi speak in the name of women but do not represent them. They have become totalitarian themselves in dictating what a woman should be and how she should behave. Their negative Paul sides have also been projected into the educational system in women's studies college courses and in the politically correct movement on college campuses. In the politically correct movement, the objective rational Paul aspect of the masculine principle in a woman is put aside in favor of political correctness or the negative expression of the inner Paul in the mass mind. Political correctness or my ego's need to make myself good is considered to be more important than the truth or scientific correctness. Gender feminists also developed women's studies on campuses which serve more to recruit students into their cause than provide for real intellectual study of women. There is also the suggestion by these feminists that a government agency should be set up to make sure our educational system should become more gender neutral or that it should foster gender-equitable education. Currently this gender re-education appears to be more involved in denying differences between the masculine and feminine principles.

As we saw with our inner Samson and David aspects of the masculine principle, Paul's final destination is to be disconnected from one's own ego needs and demands and connected with one's inner feminine principle. When the intellectual or head aspect of Paul and the heart of the feminine are not split but combined, Paul can manifest rational discrimination and a logical approach and thereby communicate in the word, the voice of the heart and our deepest intuitions.

Chapter 5

MASCULINITY TO FEMININITY: JESUS

As I walked through the circus, I saw a dark tent with a sign in front. The sign announced palm reading for sixty dollars. And when I walked in, I saw an older lady sitting behind a crystal ball. She had deep eyes and large round earrings dangling at her cheeks. She took my hand and began her tale of my life.

How is it some women have premonitions and read palms for good or bad?

I feel this is a strange night. I have a premonition that you shouldn't go on your date. Why don't you stay here with your brother and me? I read your father's horoscope today, and it says that he shouldn't go into business for himself. Maybe I should go into business myself.

Why is this woman preventing the development of her family? Is she really concerned for their welfare or merely ensnaring them with her intuitive knowings?

I can't believe what was said at the church dinner tonight. I thought by coming to church, I could be away from the pagans of the world. Surely, the people there won't be in heaven with me. I guess I'm among the few who really understand what the Christian religion means.

Is this woman truly religious or is she merely self-righteous? What do these women, the Medium and the Self-Righteous Woman, have in common with each other? Their feminine behavior is distorted by their negative spiritual inner man who is under the control of their ego needs and cut off from their positive feminine aspects. Let's look at this aspect of our inner masculine side.

This inner man is the incarnation of meaning. He is the mediator of religious experience whereby life takes on new meaning. He points beyond the physical world, an outward visible sign to a transcendent world, an inward invisible spirit. He connects a woman to her own inner spiritual reality or I AM Presence. For the Christian woman, Jesus represents this incarnation of meaning and is her guide to spiritual awareness. Rather than historically following the life of Jesus, let's look at the characteristics that define this aspect of our inner masculine side. That Jesus is the incarnation of meaning and an inner guide to spiritual wholeness can be seen in the following scriptures from the Bible.

I am the way, the truth, and the life; no man cometh unto the Father, but by me. John 14:6

...I am the light of the world: he that followeth me shall not walk in darkness, but shall have the light of life. John 8:12

...When ye have lifted up the Son of Man, then shall ye know that I am he, and that I do nothing of myself; but as my Father hath taught me, I speak these things. John 8:28

Jesus brought a new life, one beyond mere physical being.

> ...Verily, verily, I say unto thee, Except a man be born of
> water and of the Spirit, he cannot enter into the kingdom
> of God. That which is born of flesh is flesh; and that which
> is born of the Spirit is spirit. Marvel not I said unto thee,
> Ye must be born again. John 3:5-7

> And this is the will of Him that sent me, that everyone who
> seeth the Son, and believeth in him, may have everlasting
> life and I will raise him up at the last day. John 6:40

> ...I am the resurrection and the life: he that believeth in
> me, though he were dead, yet shall he live. And whosoever
> liveth and believeth in me shall not die. John 11:25-26

Many New Testament scriptures show how Jesus helped women transcend the physical and open to new spiritual understanding in their lives. To the woman of Samaria, Jesus revealed "God is Spirit." As He sat beside a well, He saw a worldly woman from Samaria drawing water, and He spoke to her saying, "Give me drink" (John 4: 7). And the woman of Samaria answered, "How is it that thou, being a Jew, askest drink of me, which am a woman of Samaria? for the Jews have no dealings with the Samaritan" (John 4:9). Jesus answered her, "If thou knowest the gift of God, and who it is that saith to thee, give me to drink, thou wouldest have asked of him, and he would have given thee living water" (John 4:10). The woman of Samaria was puzzled. Turning, she said to Jesus, "Sir, thou hast nothing to draw with, and the well is deep: from whence then hast thou that living water?" (John 4:11). Then she questioned Him further, "Art thou greater than our father Jacob, which gave us the well?" (John 4:12). Jesus answered her and said, "Whosoever drinketh of the water that I shall give him shall never thirst; but the water that I shall give him shall be in him a well of water springing up unto everlasting life" (John 4:14). And this worldly woman of Samaria was transported to a new level, and she longed to know more. She said to Jesus, "Sir, give me this water, that I thirst not, neither come hither to draw" (John 4: 15). Jesus then revealed to this woman what her past was in saying, "Thou hast had five husbands; and he whom thou now hast is not thy husband: in that saidst thou truly" (John 4: 18). This woman of Samaria then perceived that Jesus was a prophet. And Jesus said to her, "God is a Spirit, and they that worship Him must worship Him in spirit and in truth" (John 4: 24). To her, He had spoken that tremendous truth, the foundation of our knowledge of God. Jesus had asked for water, which was temporal, but He had, in turn, given her the eternal gift of spiritual fountains of the soul. And this woman of Samaria was transformed, and she said to Him, "I know that the Messiah cometh, which is called Christ: when he is come, he will tell us all things" (John 4:25). And Jesus said to her, "I that speak unto thee am he" (John 4:26). And she left her water pot and ran forth into the city to tell others. "Come, see a man, which told me all things that ever I did: is not this the Christ?" (John 4: 29).

To Martha of Bethany, Jesus revealed, "I am the Resurrection and the Life." Jesus often went to Bethany to visit Martha and her sister, Mary. They urged Him to come there when their brother, Lazarus, first was stricken ill, but Jesus was on a mission beyond the Jordan, and He delayed two days in returning to Bethany. After He had the premonition that His friend Lazarus was dead, He returned hurriedly to awaken Lazarus, as He explained, from his sleep. Martha, ever up and doing, was the first to go forth to meet Jesus. And she said, "Lord, if thou hadst been here, my brother would not have died" (John 11: 21). Martha was a believing woman and declared earnestly, "I know that even now, whatsoever thou wilt ask of God, God will give thee" (John 11:22). When Jesus told Martha that her brother would rise again, she told Him that she was sure that he would in the resurrection at the last day. Then Jesus answered her with great spiritual truth: "I am the resurrection, and the life: he that believeth in me, though he were dead, yet shall he live: And whosoever liveth and believeth in me shall never die" (John 11: 25-26).

And to Mary Magdalene, Jesus revealed, "I ascend unto my Father and your Father" (John 20: 17). When Jesus arose from the tomb, where He had been laid after being nailed to the Cross, and Mary Magdalene stood alone, weeping, that first morning at His sepulcher, she saw His body changing from its old form into a new form. "Tell them that I must shortly ascend," He said to her. And Mary Magdalene rushed forth to tell His disciples that she had seen Him rise.

Jesus revealed some of His most astonishing revelations to women and spoke to them during a time in history when such discussions with women were not acceptable. This can be seen in the last four lines of the Gospel of St. Thomas found in James Robinson's *The Nag Hammadi Library*. Here Simon Peter is reported to have said to them: "Let Mary go out from among us, because women are not worthy of the Life." Jesus was reported to have stood firm as a woman's spiritual guide in His response to Simon Peter saying, "See, I shall lead her, so that I will make her male, that she too may become a living spirit resembling you males. For every woman who makes herself male will enter the Kingdom of Heaven." This passage does not mean that a woman is to be a man. Rather, she must become aware of her inner man, Jesus, and allow Him to help her enter the Kingdom or connect with her I AM Presence. So where is this kingdom that Jesus speaks about located? In an earlier part of the Gospel of St. Thomas, Jesus points to where this kingdom can be found.

> Jesus said: If those who lead you say to you: "See, the Kingdom is in Heaven." then the birds of the heaven will precede you. If they say to you: It is in the sea, then the fish will precede you. But the Kingdom is within you and it is without you. If you know yourselves, then you will be known and you will know that you are the sons of the Living Father. But if you do not know yourselves, then you are in poverty and you are poverty.

Just as Jesus transformed the world in past historical times, so too within each woman He can transform her life. He is the inner light, the guide to the "image of God" planted within each woman.

> That was the true Light, which lighteth every man that cometh into the world...But as many as received him, to them gave he power to become the sons of God, even to them that believe on his name. John 1:9-12

And from the Book of Mary in the *Nag Hammad: Library of the Secret Gnostic* Writings of ancient Egypt Jesus says:

> Beware that no one lead you astray, saying, "Lo here!" or "Lo there!" For the Son of Man is within you. Follow after Him!

Jesus also points to the Kingdom within in the Gospel of Luke.

> ...The Kingdom of God cometh not with observation: Neither shall they say, Lo Here! Or, lo there! For, behold, the Kingdom of God is within you. Luke 17:20-21

If a woman allows her inner Jesus to perform His function of connecting her with the image of God within her or her inner I AM Presence; she can be transformed spiritually and "all these things shall be added unto you (Matthew 6:33 and Luke 12: 31)." When we open our hearts to God, we are told in Psalm 36:9 that we connect with the "fountain of life" itself—"For with thee is the fountain of life: in thy light shall we see light." When we connect with the image of God within us, we are connecting with the "fountain of life" and therefore we receive all wisdom, all knowledge, and "all things that pertain to life." We gain powers to produce miracles in the world and to command and control nature like Moses, Elijah, Elisha, Saint Paul, and Jesus did in the Bible. Emotionally our connection with our I AM Presence allows us to manifest the fruits of the Holy Spirit: love, self-control joy, peace, long-suffering, gentleness, faith, and meekness. The Old Testament story of the Queen of Sheba and King Solomon, according to Rivkah Kluger in her book *Psyche and Bible*, is an excellent example of a woman being transformed by a man in the outer world. Consider the character of King Solomon:

> And God gave Solomon wisdom and very much understanding, and largeness of heart, even as the sand that is on the seashore. And Solomon's wisdom excelled the wisdom of all the children of the east country, and all the wisdom of Egypt. For he was wiser than all men... and his fame was in all nations round about. And he spake three thousand proverbs: and his songs were a thousand and five. And he spake of trees, from the cedar tree that is in Lebanon even unto the hyssop that springeth out of the wall: he spake also of beasts, and of fowl, and of creeping things, and of fish. And there came from all peoples to hear the wisdom of Solomon, from all kings of the earth, which had heard of his wisdom. I Kings 4:29-34

Then the Queen of Sheba comes:

> And when the queen of Sheba heard of the fame of Solomon concerning the name of the Lord, she came to test him with hard questions...And Solomon answered all her questions: there was not any thing hid from the king, which he told her not... And she said to the king, it was a true report that I heard in my own land of thy acts and of thy wisdom... thy wisdom and prosperity exceedeth the fame which I heard... So she turned and went to her own country, she and her servants. I Kings 10:1-13

Rivkah Kluger points out that the Queen of Sheba came to prove King Solomon with hard questions. The Hebrew word "nasa" means to test and also to tempt. And "hidot" not only means hard questions but riddles. She came to test him with riddles. This, according to Kluger, suggests a power struggle. King Solomon, however, proves himself too wise, and the Queen of Sheba bows before him. That is, she accepts his wisdom. But the Queen of Sheba does not display negative feelings in her defeat. Rather, she seems to have a longing for something higher, a longing for a wisdom that transcends hers, for she says, "Blessed be the Lord thy God, who delighted in thee on the throne of Israel. Because the Lord loved Israel forever, therefore made he thee king, to execute justice and righteousness" (I Kings 10:9). This suggests, according to Kluger, that the Queen of Sheba would like to always be close to King Solomon in order to participate in his wisdom. Her submission deepens into a full acceptance of Solomon's religion. "And King Solomon gave unto the Queen of Sheba all her desire…" (I Kings 10:12). Thus, in this story, King Solomon serves as a type of mediator of new religious meaning in the Queen of Sheba's life, just as each woman's inner man Jesus can provide this in her life. Though King Solomon was a wise and great man, Jesus said,

> The queen of the south shall rise up in the judgment with this generation, and shall condemn it: for she came from the uttermost parts of the earth to hear the wisdom of Solomon; and behold a greater than Solomon is here.
> Matthew 12:42

By connecting a woman to her I AM Presence and thus the "fountain of life" itself, Jesus acts in the inner world like Solomon did in the outer world with Sheba and opens her to seeing all things—past, present, and future—and thus developing prophetic abilities. Connection with her I AM Presence also ensures that she gains divine wisdom that is greater than Solomon's.

The wisdom of God and prophetic abilities that Jesus opens in a woman can be found in several women of the Bible. Huldah of the Old Testament provides a good example of a woman who allowed her inner

Jesus to bring forth divine wisdom. She was known in Jerusalem for her prophetic powers. King Josiah sent five of his personal messengers to her with the Book of the Law, which had been discovered in Jerusalem. He had faith in Huldah's spiritual powers, and he wanted her to tell him whether the book was genuine or not.

> And she answered them, Thus saith the Lord God of Israel, Tell ye the man who sent you to me, Thus saith the Lord, Behold, I will bring evil upon this place, and upon its inhabitants thereof, even all the curses that are written in the book which they have read before the king of Judah. Because they have forsaken me, and have burned incense unto other gods, that they might provoke me to anger with all the works of their hands; therefore, my wrath shall be poured out upon this place, and shall not be quenched. And as the King of Judah, who sent you to inquire of the Lord, so shall ye say unto him, Thus saith the Lord God of Israel concerning the words which thou hast heard: Because thine heart was tender, and thou didst humble thyself before God, when thou hearest his words against this place, and against its inhabitants, and humblest thyself before me, and didst tear thy clothes, and weep before me, I have heard thee also, saith the Lord. Behold, I will gather thee to thy fathers, and thou shalt be gathered to thy grave in peace; neither shall thine eyes see all the evil that I will bring upon this place, and upon the inhabitants of the same. So, they brought the king word again. II Chronicles 34:23-28

In this short passage Huldah uses the phrase, "Thus saith the Lord," four different times. This suggests that she thought of herself only as a channel through which God spoke rather than taking personal credit for her prophetic powers. This behavior shows that she was not under the control of her ego since it always seeks its own praise and admiration. Here Huldah not only confirms the authenticity of the Book of the Law but also prophesies concerning the future saying that the Lord would bring evil upon Judah because the people had forsaken Him. So aroused was King Josiah with what Huldah had revealed that he set in motion the words written in the Book of the Covenant. He and his people went to the house of the Lord, and there they made a pledge to walk once more in God's commandments as revealed in the Book of the Law—a good part of which appears in the Book of Deuteronomy in the Bible.

The witch of Endor provides another example of a woman with prophetic powers. During a time of desperation King Saul consulted this medium who lived in a cave.

> And when Saul saw the host of the Philistines, he was afraid, and his heart greatly trembled. And when Saul inquired of the Lord, the Lord answered him not... Then said Saul unto his servants, Seek me a woman who is a medium, that I may go to her, and inquire of her. And his servants said to him, Behold, there is a medium at Endor.
> I Samuel 28:5-7

The scene in which Saul seeks the help of this medium is intensely dramatic. The desperate king, conscious that Divine favor had departed from him, and terrified by the powers massed against him, sinks into despair. He thinks of Samuel and wishes to see him. So, in the darkness of the night, King Saul, disguised in a long cloak, goes to the dwelling of the wise woman of Endor.

The witch of Endor receives her mysterious visitors with caution, since Saul himself had driven out the spiritualists and mediums from Israel. But King Saul quiets her fear of prosecution.

> Then said the woman, whom shall I bring up unto thee? And he said, bring me up Samuel... and Samuel said to Saul...tomorrow shalt thou and thy sons be with me...
> I Samuel 28:11-19

The voice brought forth told King Saul of his death the following day. And the witch of Endor rose to a noble stature. She comforted King Saul and tried to strengthen him to meet his fate.

> Now, therefore, I pray thee harken, thou also unto the voice of thine handmaid, and let me set a morsel of bread before thee; and eat, that thou mayest have strength, when thou goest on thy way. Samuel 28:22

In the New Testament, Pilate's wife showed prophetic insight in the dream she had just prior to Jesus' Crucifixion.

> When he was seated on the judgment seat, his wife sent unto him, saying, have thou nothing to do with that just man: for I have suffered many things this day in a dream because of him. Matthew 27:19

Pilate's wife had this dream the night that armed men, working for the chief priests, had arrested Jesus. And she sent a message by a servant imploring her husband not to condemn Jesus. When her inner Jesus connected her with her I AM Presence, she became aware of the approaching evil. These seeds in her unconscious flowered into a dream, and she tried to save her husband from his terrible decision to put Jesus to death. Her intervention caused Pilate to hesitate and once more to give the mob a choice between Jesus and Barabbas, but they chose to crucify Jesus. Not only was Pilate's wife right about the innocence of Jesus, but her husband was also headed for disaster. His administration ended abruptly, and it was reported that he was banished to the south of France and ultimately committed suicide.

Now let's look at the Medium and Self-Righteous type of women in which the spiritual inner man serves a negative rather than positive role. What has happened in the Medium and witches who use their powers selfishly for evil and destruction? The story of Lucifer suggests an answer to this question.

> How art thou fallen from heaven, O Lucifer, son of the morning! How art thou cut down to the ground, who didst weaken the nations!
>
> For thou hast said in thine heart, I will ascend into heaven, I will exalt my throne above the stars of God: I will also sit upon the mount of the congregation, in the sides of the north, I will ascend above the heights of the clouds, I will be like the most High. Isaiah 14:12-14

Lucifer, who was created by God and anointed for a special position of authority, rejected God. With the statement, "I will," Lucifer separated himself from God and built his own kingdom of specialness. His ego inflation can easily be seen in the statement, "I will exalt my throne above the stars of God." Lucifer is saying that he will use the powers given to him by God to build his own kingdom or to satisfy his own ego needs and desires. And what are the characteristics of Lucifer? He is deceitful, wicked, ensnaring, devouring and a liar.

> But I fear, lest by any means, as the serpent beguiled Eve through his subtilty ... II Corinthians 11:3
>
> I write unto you, fathers, because ye have known him that is from the beginning. I write unto you, young men, because we have overcome the wicked one ... I John 2:13
>
> Moreover, he must have a good report of them which are without, lest he fall into reproach and the snare of the devil. I Timothy 3:7

Be sober, be vigilant; because your adversary, the devil, as a roaring lion walketh about, seeking whom he may devour. I Peter 5:8

But if our gospel be hid it is hid to them that are lost: In whom the god of this age hath blinded the minds of them who believe not, lest the light of the glorious gospel of Christ, who is the image of God should shine unto them. II Corinthians 4:3-4

Ye are of your father the devil, and the lusts of your father ye will do. He was a murderer from the beginning, and abode not in the truth, because there is no truth in him. When he speaketh a lie, he speaketh of his own: for he is a liar, and the father of it. John 8:44

Like Lucifer, if a woman listens to the voice of her ego, she will disconnect from God and the kingdom of heaven within her and the powers of her spiritual inner man will serve her ego rather than God. She will see these powers as her own and use them to satisfy her ego needs and build her own kingdom of specialness like Lucifer. Her inner man becomes a wizard entrapping and destroying others. Unlike Huldah, she is inflated with pride and uses her powers for evil. Unlike the witch of Endor, she does not comfort or nourish, rather she devours and destroys. Being disconnected from the I AM Presence within her, she doesn't love or relate but ensnares and hates. Unlike Pilate's wife, who used her powers to try to prevent the death of Jesus and the destruction of her husband, a woman possessed by this negative inner man may have a bewitching and destructive effect on her family. She may stifle the development of potentials of which they are not even aware of. She sees others' talents still residing in their unconscious and often foresees what shape these talents might take. She may then prevent these talents from developing or take them to be her own, thus robbing others of experiences that belong to them.

In recent years there has been a move among some feminists in the women's movement to return to the mother goddess myths and religions. Christianity is labeled as a religion dominated by the patriarchy and not meeting a woman's needs. I have often wondered if a woman's negative spiritual man may be leading them backward into darkness rather than forward into enlightenment.

In the Self-Righteous Woman, Lucifer operates under the guise of being religious, but his true nature can easily be seen in her behavior. Her brand of religion involves condemnation and separation not forgiveness and connection. The heart of God cannot be found in her scriptures or behavior. She may even neglect her family in pursuit of her religion. It's as if her religion is separate from her family and their needs. Such a woman tries to behave in a "Christ-like" manner, but she doesn't have a real relationship with her inner Jesus or connection with the heart of God and therefore her behavior is more like a pantomime of what she thinks Christ would say or do. All of this self-righteous behavior really is an attempt to cover up deeper feelings of unworthiness, a sense of lack, and unlovability. A sense of unworthiness and guilt always lies under pride or arrogance. The voice of a woman's ego is always negative but it can speak negatively in a variety of ways. It can tell a woman that she is ugly, weak, helpless, inadequate, alone, unlovable, unworthy or somehow not just right. In essence, this ego voice tells a woman that she is not good and does not have the Holy Spirit or God within her and to believe that she does is labeled as arrogant by this voice. Although a woman's belief in this voice gives it all the power that it has over her; she, like Eve many years ago, is beguiled by this serpent ego voice inside of her mind. She then uses her inner man to build a kingdom of specialness over this foundation of guilt and unworthiness not recognizing that her sense of unworthiness is but an illusory belief fostered by her own ego. Some women live their lives in this loop of negativity never actualizing the positive depths of their femininity.

In both the Medium and Self-Righteous types of women, the inner spiritual man functions negatively like Lucifer turning her into a witch or fooling her with self-righteous religiosity. This negative functioning occurs when the powers of this inner man are distorted by a woman's ego desires. As was the case for the inner men in the preceding chapters, a woman's conscious awareness of this negative manifestation must precede any attempt at correction and positive redirection.

First a woman must allow herself to become aware of her ego identification with the wrong-minded ego and how she is using her spiritual inner man negatively. She then allows and welcomes Jesus to perform His proper function of mediating the spiritual. As the scriptures below point out, Jesus will come and transform when He is truly welcome.

> And I say unto you, Ask, and it shall be given you; seek, and ye shall find; knock, and it shall be opened unto you. Luke 11:9

> Behold I stand at the door, and knock: if any man hear my voice, and open the door, I will come in to him, and will sup with him, and he with me. Revelations 3:20

We can't have it both ways. We can either listen to the voice of the ego, which causes our inner spiritual guide or Jesus inner man to turn negative and distort the expression of our femininity in the world or we can release His connection with our ego needs and desires. This is accomplished by applying the Law of Forgiveness that Jesus introduced during His ministry. The Law of Forgiveness is based on the feminine form of "letting go" activity, which simply involves mentally directing the ego to leave and then letting this voice go. In past historical time, Jesus modeled this behavior when Satan tempted him in the wilderness following His baptism by John the Baptist. Jesus did not attack Satan or feel sorry for himself for being tempted; rather he applied the Law of Forgiveness and let Satan's attack go. Jesus said, "...Get thee hence, Satan: for it is written, Thou shalt worship the Lord, thy God, and him only shalt thou serve" (Matthew 4:10) and "Then the devil leaveth him…" (Matthew 4:11). Like Jesus did so long ago, we can apply the Law of Forgiveness and let attacks against us by others and by our own egos go instead of taking them in and attacking ourselves with them. And as we let go of the negative song of the ego and affirm our I AM Presence we can stand resolute in our connection to the I AM Presence. Our inner Jesus can now function positively and connect us to the "fountain of life" within and thereby restoring our spiritual powers.

Chapter 6

TRULY FEMININE

> And the seventh angel sounded; and there were great voices in heaven, saying, The Kingdoms of this world are become the kingdoms of our Lord... And there appeared a great wonder in heaven; a woman clothed with the sun, and the moon under her feet, and upon her head a crown of twelve stars... Revelation 11:15-12:1

In the Book of Revelation by John, there's a good image of the truly feminine woman. She is described as "a woman clothed with the sun, and the moon under her feet." The symbols of the moon and the sun are important in understanding the nature of this woman. In many religions, legends, and myths the moon has been associated with the feminine principle. If we consider the characteristics of the moon's behavior, it's easy to see why this is so. The moon is reflecting, it waxes and wanes like the feminine form of activity discussed in Chapter I. On the other hand, the sun has generally been taken as an image of the masculine because it symbolizes the light of consciousness and its activity is steady and penetrates darkness. These characteristics are typically associated with the masculine principle. Thus, in John's revelation, we see a woman standing on the moon or standing firmly in her femininity, but she is clothed by the sun. That is, her masculine side is in balance with her feminine side thus resulting in a fully conscious woman who is whole, harmonious, and is in a loving relationship with others and the Divine.

This new woman is not a pseudo-man. She is not unconsciously identified with or possessed by her inner men. In the preceding four chapters we have seen how our inner men when disconnected from aspects of the feminine principle and serving one's ego needs can negatively impact a woman's behavior and distort the true expression of her femininity. His negative functioning can turn women into judges, social climbers, bosses, mermaid women, spinning tops, scholarly women, patriarchal women, good or nagging wives, witches, and self-righteous women.

However, when we become aware of our inner men, and redirect their energies, they can become positive forces in our lives. This redirection involves disconnecting them from serving our ego needs and desires and connecting them with various aspects of our femininity as well as the I AM Presence or the image of God within us. We can see this in the actual lives of Samson, David, Paul, and Jesus. According to biblical accounts each of these men got caught in their own ego needs but then had an encounter with the Divine, which radically changed their lives so they were able to serve God and complete their missions in life. Samson, whose name means "little sun", was declared by an angel to be a man set apart from other men because of his religious mission. He lost sight of his spiritual mission when he encountered Delilah who betrayed him by revealing the secret of his strength and power to the Philistines. Samson told Delilah that, "if I am shaved, then my strength will go from me." She then told the Philistines who shaved off "the seven locks of his head" and he lost his power and strength. The Philistines also put out his eyes but "the hair of his head began to grow again" and he recovered his strength while imprisoned. Then, one day, the Philistines brought forth Samson "to make sport for them" and he called to God to strengthen him so that he could avenge the

Philistines for blinding him and he pulled down the pillars and destroyed all who were there.

In the story of David, we can see dynamics similar to the story of Samson. David, who dearly loved God, became so enraptured with Bathsheba that he committed adultery with her and later had her husband murdered. He broke his relationship with God to follow his ego desires but later repented and was forgiven by God. In the New Testament, the story of Paul again shows how an encounter with the Divine can radically change one's life. Armed with authority of the chief priest, Paul started for the city of Damascus, intending to stamp out the Christian infection there. But unbeknownst to Paul, this journey was to change his life and the course of history.

> And as he journeyed, he came near Damascus: and suddenly there shone around about him a light from heaven; And he fell to the earth, and heard a voice saying unto him, Saul, Saul, why persecutest thou me?... I am Jesus, whom thou persecutest... And he trembling and astonished said, Lord, what wilt thou have me to do? And the Lord said unto him, Arise, and go into the city, and it shall be told thee what thou must do... And Saul arose from the earth, and when his eyes were opened, he saw no man: but they led him by the hand and brought him into Damascus... Ananias...putting his hand on him said... receive thy sight and be filled with the Holy Spirit...And he preached Christ in the synagogues, that he is the Son of God. Acts 9:3-20

From this very personal encounter with the Divine, Paul shifted away from his ego needs and the collective traditions of his faith and turned to the light of his own inner authority. An inner authority based on a personal encounter with the Divine. And with this light of consciousness, he became the bearer of the Word unto many nations. He claimed that God had committed to him the mission of taking Christ's teachings to the

Gentiles. He and Barnabas set out to evangelize the Gentiles while Peter and the other disciples were focusing on a similar mission to the Jews. The Book of Acts narrates three different "missionary journeys" that took Paul into many cities and through incredible adventures. He taught the new converts and helped them organize for their new life in Christ and stayed as long as he felt he could and then moved on to other places.

In the life of Jesus, we see following his baptism by John the Baptist "the Spirit of God descending like a dove, and lighting upon him" and "then was Jesus led up by the spirit into the wilderness to be tested by the devil." Following these events, Jesus began his three-year ministry. Jesus promised His disciples that he would "pray to the Father, and he shall give you another Comforter, that he may abide with you forever" John 14:16. Just as the Comforter or Holy Spirit was ushered in by Jesus in past historical times so too one's inner Jesus' aspect will bring forth a connection with the Divine or I AM Presence within and thus the fruits of this spirit.

In the lives of Samson, David, Paul, and Jesus reported in the Bible, we can see how each one is changed by an encounter with the Divine that resulted in the fulfillment of their missions on Earth. Now, if we view these biblical stories intrapsychically, it suggests that our inner Samson, David, Paul, and Jesus masculine aspects can be spiritualized. We have seen the ways in which these aspects of our inner men can be perverted and negatively affect our feminine behavior. But their final purpose, both in historical biblical times and within each of us, is to be disconnected from ego needs, balanced with various aspects of the feminine principle, and thus reconnected in a harmonious loving relationship with others as well as with the Divine in the full bloom of conscious awareness.

By becoming aware of our inner Jesus and disconnecting Him from our ego needs and demands, He can properly perform His function of connecting us to the image of God within us and thereby spiritualize our feminine aspects and restore our spiritual powers. Rivkah Kluger, in an unpublished manuscript entitled "Women in the Old Testament," shows that an encounter with the Divine can spiritualize our mothering instincts. She illustrates with the lives of Sarah, Rachel, and Hannah how the natural maternal instincts are broadened beyond the activity of giving physical birth to a child. Sarah was married to Abraham whom the Lord had told would "be a mother of nations; kings of people shall be of her." However, this destined tribal mother was at first barren. She suffered greatly from her barrenness and inability to become a mother. Her whole meaning in life seemed tied to her maternal instincts. Desperate to have children, Sarah's inner Samson, which was connected with her ego needs and demands, devised her own plan by suggesting to Abraham that he have children by her handmaid, Hagar. The story of Hagar shows Sarah's jealousy of the other woman, not as a rival for her husband's love but as the woman who has given birth to his son. Sarah even disbelieved and laughed at God's promise that she would have a child beyond the typical age for physical motherhood. But as her desire to become a mother moves toward fulfillment Sarah opens her heart and sees that this child was a God-sent miracle.

We see a similar trend in the story of Rachel and her sister Leah. Leah, like Hagar, is identified with the mother role. She is the fruitful one, whereas Rachel is barren at first. Leah gives birth to six of the twelve promised sons, and being a mother is her only satisfaction. For Rachel, motherhood is, as it was for Sarah, a problem at first. She is barren and is jealous of Leah, but then, as with Sarah, her wish to become a mother is fulfilled. She found, as did Sarah, that feminine fulfillment comes through a conscious encounter with God. Thus, Rachel grew into spiritual motherhood, which raised her beyond the natural mother, and she remains alongside the much younger figure of Queen Esther as an honored and beloved mother of the Jewish people.

In the character of Hannah, we again see a woman who deeply desired to be a mother but was barren. Her husband Elkanah's other wife,

Peninnah, did have children, and she provoked Hannah, "provoked her sore, for to make her fret, because the Lord had shut up her womb" (I Samuel 1:6). Though Hannah was deeply hurt by Peninnah's taunting, she had the strength to turn to God. And she vowed a promise and said, "O Lord of hosts, if thou wilt indeed look on the affliction of thine handmaid, and remember me, and not forget thine handmaid, but wilt give unto thine handmaid a male child, then I will give him unto the Lord all the days of his life, and there shall be no razor come upon his head" (I Samuel 1: 11). Hannah's prayer was answered, and she gave birth to Samuel. And Hannah kept her promise to the Lord by giving Samuel to him. So again, we have a woman blocked in her role as a natural mother but who solves this problem by turning to God. Hannah shows greater maturity than Sarah. Her inner Samson was not distorted by her own ego needs or demands as she did not devise her own plan to have a child; rather, she turned to God to fulfill this aspect of her femininity.

We can also spiritualize our other inner men by disconnecting them from our ego needs, balancing them with certain aspects of the feminine principle, and reconnecting them in a harmonious, loving relationship with God in full conscious awareness. This also paves the way to use these inner masculine attributes to help complete our own mission in life and the implementation of the Divine plan. Marianne Williamson, in her books entitled *A Return to Love* and *A Woman's Worth*, evidences a contemporary example of how our Jesus inner man can transform and give new meaning to life by connecting us to the image of God within us and in turn this connection spiritualizes our other inner men—Samson, David, and Paul. In *A Woman's Worth*, you can see the development of different manifestations of her inner masculine side and their transformations as Williamson searches for her feminine worth. Like many women she begins her search for her Samson masculine power side by looking for it in men. She says, "I use to think that I needed a powerful man, someone who could protect me from harshness and evils of the world." She was unaware of her inner Samson and in fact projected it onto her outer man. At this point in her development, Williamson believed that her safety was outside of herself. Safety was derived from associating herself with the external power as seen in men in the world rather than from her connection with her inner Samson masculine aspect.

External power has also been associated with having material abundance and worldly position. The search for this type of power was also seen in Georgette Mosbacher in her book *Feminine Force.* But with Marianne Williamson we see the realization that power is within us. She discovers that "until we own our own power, we will constantly seek it in others, particularly in men, and power sought that way never saves us, it destroys us." She realizes "internal power has less to do with money and worldly position and more to do with emotional expansiveness, spirituality, and conscious living." This leads her to look for a different type of powerful man, one "who supported me in keeping on track spiritually." Internal power is seen as spiritual power. "We are lost and disconnected because we do not perceive ourselves in spiritual terms. We think of ourselves as flesh and bone, resumes and relationships, clothes and cosmetics. It's time to remember we're the daughters of God."

So here we can see how Jesus can transform our love, power, and worthiness. It does not lie outside of ourselves in men, material possessions or in worldly position. If we anchor our love, power and worthiness outside of ourselves, it will fail us and we cannot transcend the subject/object dichotomy or our separation from God. In fact, to look outside of oneself for love, power or worthiness implies and reinforces the idea that one is empty and lacking in these qualities on the inside.

At another stage in her development, Marianne Williamson tries to obtain love and self-worth by identifying with the doing energy of her David inner man. She says that she was a "father's daughter" at one time. "The way to succeed, it seemed to us, was to grow up and be just like Daddy." She further confesses, "I had seen my father's lack of emotion as strength and my mother's show of emotion as weakness." Williamson considered her "emotions were less important than her achievements, perhaps even antithetical to them." She points out "that we were taught as children ... that our value lies in what we do as opposed to who we are, we automatically switch to a masculine mode of doing, doing, doing in order to feel worthy." However, Williamson comes to realize that "the love I received in response to her achievements, if it was love at all, is not the love that warms the night."

Achievement, regardless of what kind, does not bring the type of permanent love that results from an internal sense of self-worth. Williamson translates her self-worth from one that is based on doing to one that is based on being, an aspect of the feminine mode of activity. This can easily be seen in the statement "we can't look to the world to restore our worth ... only God can crown us, and he already has." One's level of doing in the world becomes extending from the inside to the outside rather than taking from the outside to justify the inside. That is, one's doing is not an attempt to gain love, power or worthiness from one's actions in the world; instead, it's extending these qualities from oneself or I AM Presence out into the world.

And what is the truly feminine woman like? This woman who has accepted and re-directed her inner men away from her ego desires and balanced them with certain aspects of the feminine principle will form a harmonious, loving relationship with God in full conscious awareness. She is the "bearer" of the feminine principle, the Holy Spirit, into the world. Our world needs this principle to complement and balance the effects of the masculine principle. Mary, the mother of Jesus, provides a good example of a woman who was in touch with her inner men and used them in combination with the feminine principle to serve God. The angel Gabriel and her cousin Elizabeth said of her "blessed art thou among women" (Luke 1:28,42).

And in the sixth month the angel, Gabriel was sent from God unto a city in Galilee, named Nazareth, to a virgin espoused to a man whose name was Joseph, of the house of David; and the virgin's name was Mary. And the angel came in unto her, and said, Hail, thou who art highly favored, the Lord is with thee: blessed art thou among women. And when she saw him, she was troubled at his saying, and considered in her mind what manner of salutation this should be. And the angel said unto her, Fear not, Mary: for thou hast found favor with God. And, behold, thou shalt conceive in thy womb, and bring forth a son, and shalt call his name Jesus. He shall be great, and shall be called the Son of the Highest: and the Lord God shall give unto him the throne of his father David: And he shall reign over the house of Jacob forever; and of his kingdom there shall be no end... And Mary said Behold the handmaid of the Lord; be it unto me according to thy word. And the angel departed from her. Luke 1:26-38

So here we see Gabriel serving as the bridge to mediate God to Mary, just as Jesus does within each woman. Her inner David and Paul provided Mary with the ability to stand and act from an inner authority based on this divine revelation. She did not falter in acting on her inner authority, even when she knew that she must suffer the pain of criticism from those who did not understand the wonder of her approaching pregnancy. Even Joseph "was minded to put her away privately" (Matthew 1:19). With Mary, David is baptized in the sense of taking a stand for God and His plan. That is, Mary uses her inner David to act in accordance with God's will rather than using him to carry out her own ego demands. She also uses her inner David to connect her feelings in a personal relationship with God: "And Mary said, Behold the handmaid of the Lord..." (Luke 1:38).

In Mary's Magnificat we can see her inner Paul providing her with the ability to give rational form to her spiritual experience.

And Mary said, My soul doth magnify the Lord, And my spirit hath rejoiced in God my Savior. For he hath regarded the low estate of his handmaiden: for, behold, from henceforth all generations shall call me blessed. For he that is mighty hath done to me great things; and holy is his name. And his mercy is on them that fear him from generation to generation. He hath shown strength with his arm; he hath scattered the proud in the imagination of their hearts. He hath put down the mighty from their seats, and exalted them of low degree. He hath filled the hungry with good things; and the rich he hath sent empty away. He hath helped his servant Israel, in remembrance of his mercy; As he spoke to our fathers, to Abraham, and to his seed forever. Luke 1:46-55

In these moving lines, Mary praises God from her heart for his wonderful works. Here Mary shows her dedication to God and his laws.

And throughout the manifestation of Gabriel's revelation to Mary, her inner Samson provided her with strength, power, and courage to sustain Simeon's prophecy: "Yea, a sword shall pierce through thy own soul also, that the thoughts of many hearts may be revealed" (Luke 2:35). Imagine the strength it took to sustain the crucifixion of her own son.

Now there stood by the cross of Jesus his mother, and his mother's sister, Mary, the wife of Clopas, and Mary Magdalene. John 19:25

...I thirst. John 19:28

...It is finished. John 19:30

But one of the soldiers, with a spear, pierced his side, and forthwith came there out blood and water. John 19:34

Mary's inner Samson was baptized by her inner Jesus to perform this service for God, and she used his strength and courage to fulfill her feminine destiny as the mother of the Son of God.

In using each of her inner men in service of God's plan, Mary fully actualized her feminine nature and thereby used her inner men to serve and extend the feminine principle. She used both the dynamic (Samson and David) and the static (Paul and Jesus) poles of the masculine principle, which we talked about in Table 1 in Chapter 1, and fully actualized her feminine nature or the feminine principle. Like the masculine principle, the feminine principle has both a static and dynamic pole. Ann Ulanov in her book, *The Feminine in Jungian Psychology and Christian Theology*, states that Mary actualized four major forms of the feminine principle. Consider the names of praise given to Mary such as "Mother of Mercy", "Mother Most Blessed", "Mother Most Pure", "Spiritual Vessel", "Queen of Heaven", "Handmaid of the Lord", and "Virgin Most Powerful." In these names we can see the basic four structural forms that Ann Ulanov and Toni Wolff in her article "Structural Forms of the Feminine Psyche" talk about. Let's examine more closely the static and dynamic poles of the feminine principle and tie these to the various names of praise given to Mary.

In the first chapter, the static feminine was defined as inert. cold, indifferent, unseeing, gestating and waiting, ceaselessly creating, destroying, adverse to consciousness and discipline, receptive, yielding, holding, containing, emotional experiencing, intuitive, impersonal, nonindividual and collective. This static pole of the feminine provides the basis for mothering activities, but it can be positive or negative, just like our inner man can be positive or negative. Mary magnifies the positive aspect of the mother as can be seen in her titles as "Mother Most Blessed", "Mother Most Pure", and "Mother of Mercy." Mary, the mother of Jesus, nourished and protected her Son, but unlike the Clinging-Vine mother type, when she was no longer needed, she withdrew.

> And when they saw him, they were amazed and his mother said unto him, Son, why hast thou thus dealt with us? Behold, thy father and I have sought thee, sorrowing. And he said unto them, how is it that ye sought me? wist ye not that I must be about my Father's business? Luke 2:48-49

> And the multitude sat about him, and they said unto him, Behold, thy mother and thy brethren without seek for thee. And he answered them saying, Who is my mother, or my brethren? And he looked round about on them which sat about him, and said, Behold my mother and my brethren! For whosoever shall do the will of God, the same is my brother, and my sister, and my mother. Mark 3:32-35

No doubt Mary was beginning to know that, for those who live the life of the spirit, the human family bond is transcended by a wider love. Note that Mary did not insist on nourishing and protecting her son, nor did she become possessive of Him like the Clinging-Vine type of mother. Her inner Samson was not trapped in her mothering instincts. Like Hannah, Mary remained in the background while Jesus carried out his life's mission. But Jesus never forgot His mother even in the hour of His greatest suffering.

> When Jesus therefore saw his mother, and the disciple standing by, whom he loved, he saith unto his mother, Woman, behold thy son! Then saith he to the disciple, Behold thy mother! And from that hour that disciple took her unto his own home. John 19:26-27

The static pole of the feminine also provides a woman with the feminine capacity to be an intercessor as she mediates the human to the Divine and the Divine to the human. Her inner man, Jesus, releases this aspect of her feminine nature. However, as we saw in Chapter 5, there is a negative manifestation of this form of the feminine when a women's inner man takes the form of Lucifer bewitching and devouring others as well as the woman herself. The positive aspect of this feminine form can be seen in Mary's titles as "Queen of Heaven" and "Spiritual Vessel." Like Huldah, Mary was a great prophetess who remained close to the Eternal throughout her life. To Mary was given God's greatest revelation for the redemption of the world.

Mary also manifested the dynamic pole of the feminine principle. This aspect of the feminine principle involves eros, urge to unite, unify, connect with concrete people rather than with things or ideas, and get involved for the sake of personal subjective emotional union. Unlike the Mermaid Woman, Mary's inner David was connected and, in turn, connected her to her deep feminine feelings, which were manifested in her close personal relationship with Joseph as well as with God. This personal feeling relationship with God can be seen in her title as "Handmaid of the Lord." Several times Mary referred to herself as handmaid of the Lord. "And Mary said, Behold the handmaid of the Lord" (Luke 1:38). And in the Magnificat, Mary thanked God for regarding "the low estate of his handmaid" (Luke 1:48). A handmaid is a servant to another, one who is very personally dedicated to the details and needs of another. Mary never faulted as a humble handmaid of the Lord; a connotation first used by Hannah, mother of Samuel, having evolved from the word slave then to domestic servant.

Mary also shows a personal relatedness or involvement with the non-personal goals or values. This aspect of the feminine can be seen in her title as "Virgin Most Pure." According to Ann Ulanov:

> Mary as Virgin ... symbolizes the way in which a complete ordering and opening of one's life to the divine may make one intact and chaste. Chastity is the rectitude of a life which puts central commitment totally at the center and

which allows no perforations by merely peripheral or competing concerns.

Like Priscilla and Lydia, Mary's inner Paul connected her personal feelings to the goals of God and the Church. The last we see of Mary is when she was gathered with the disciples in the Upper Room in Jerusalem after Jesus' Ascension.

> These all continued with one accord in prayer and supplication, with the women, and Mary the mother of Jesus, and with his brethren. Acts 1:14

So, with Mary, we can see four forms of the feminine: Mother, Prophetess, Handmaid, and Virgin. Toni Wolf suggests that these four aspects of the feminine form two sets of opposites as illustrated in Table 2.

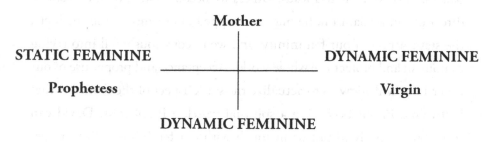

As can be seen, each pair of these feminine forms is a set of opposites: the Mother and the Handmaid are the collective and individual forms of relatedness to people; the Virgin and the Prophetess are the individual and collective forms of relatedness to non-personal values and principles. According to Toni Wolf and Ann Ulanov, every woman has all four of these aspects of the feminine. However, one will be actualized or is superior in a woman according to her nature. A woman then develops not the opposite form but one of the two auxiliary forms of the feminine.

For example, the Mother type typically develops the Virgin or Prophetess rather than the handmaid form of the feminine. According to Toni Wolf, if the gradual integration of the next structural form does not take place, the original one will be exaggerated and turn negative. With further development, the third form will have to be dealt with. This one usually lies on the same axis as the second but has more of a shadowy character and can be less easily reconciled with the first one. The fourth form of the feminine causes the greatest difficulty and generally cannot be lived out concretely since it represents a great contrast to the original character. According to Toni Wolf, the integration of the fourth structural form is an approach to wholeness, a task that typically requires a lifetime.

Toni Wolf discusses only the structural forms of the feminine and does not deal with how the masculine or our inner men are involved in their manifestation. As previously pointed out, the feminine principle is actualized through the realization and proper utilization of our inner men: Samson, David, Paul and Jesus. Unless we become aware of and properly direct our inner Samson, he may get trapped in our mothering instincts, the static aspect of our femininity, and we unconsciously fall into trying to nourish and protect the whole world. Acceptance and proper use of our inner Jesus will allow us to actualize the static aspect of the feminine that is involved in our becoming a spiritual vessel, a Prophetess. David can function positively to put us in touch with our feminine feelings to get personally involved as the Handmaid. And our inner Paul can connect our feelings to non-personal values and principles, which allow us to become the chaste Virgin. Thus, David and Paul help us actualize the dynamic pole of the feminine principle while Samson and Paul help in the actualization of the static pole of the feminine.

Now let's review what the women's movement has said to women about the nature and actualization of the feminine principle. American feminism according to Dr. Sommers has had several waves washing through the culture and bringing about many changes in our views about femininity. The first wave, according to Sommers, began 150 years ago and focused on achieving legal, political and educational equity for women. As Elizabeth Cady Stanton, a major leader of equity or mainstream feminism, said before the New York State Legislature in 1854, "we need no other protection than that which your present laws secure to you." This first wave achieved a greater degree of equality between masculinity and femininity as evidenced in some of the legal, political, and educational changes they brought about.

The second wave of feminism which began in the mid-sixties sees women as being caught in a sex/gender system of male domination. According to Gloria Steinem, "all patriarchal cultures idealize, sexualize and generally prefer weak women." The view here is that our male-dominated society forces us to play sex gender roles. The second wave "gender" feminists are angry and intent on fighting. Dr. Sommers maintains that these "gender" feminists are "preoccupied with their own sense of hurt and their own feelings of embattlement and siege." She suggests that these feminists are "so sensitive that they need the smelling salts" that were used by women many years ago "when they fainted in response to male vulgarity." Susan Faludi, Gloria Steinem, and many women in the NOW organization are representative of the 'gender" feminists, but grass root women do not support the views of these feminists. Georgette Mosbacher in the *Feminine Force* warns:

> Watch out for the theoreticians of anger who will try to dissuade you from this. Watch out for the women who argue that beauty is a myth perpetuated to keep us down and that the pursuit of beauty is evidence of a backlash against women unleashed by male capitalists out of greed and fear. Watch out for people who tell you that you don't know how to listen to your inner voice and that your choices are dictated by other people who are making you miserable.

Dr. Sommers calls for a new direction for feminism that is not "at odds with the real aspirations and values of most American women" and does not "undermine the cause of true equality."

Naomi Wolf, in her book *Fire with Fire*, departs from the extreme "gender" or victim feminism that she espoused in *The Beauty Myth* and calls women to a new third wave of feminism that she has labeled as power feminism. She speaks for a more ideologically flexible feminism in the 1990's that does not require women to follow the rigid dictates of conduct and beliefs required by the "gender" feminists of the second wave. This Wolf believes would help bring the majority of grass root women back into the women's movement. She still believes that men will have to be "forcefully pressed to yield power" but does maintain that "the fight against sexism must not lead to hating men." She believes that "if women are to take their rightful power, there will have to be a vast surge in organizational activities." She calls women to form power groups and thereby create an alternative female power structure that is not dependent on men and their networks. She sees a woman's power as lying outside of herself in gaining and using such things as money, education, voting and consuming "to get what she determines that she needs."

Dr. Sommers states that, "Wolf's power feminism turns out to be a version of the classically liberal mainstream feminism with the addition of some contemporary 'feel good' themes." It seems to me that although Wolf talks some about our power or Samson within, she focuses primarily on gaining power in terms of the external world of material things and using it to be a political activist. Her work reminds me of Georgette Mosbacher's *Feminine Force* in that both are looking for power externally in the world. Wolf's new work, like that of Mosbacher, appears to reflect a projected attempt to deal with the power aspect of her inner Samson side. Samson's power is projected out into the world of people and things and then these are sought in order to gain a sense of power. Wolf also talks about power feminism as a humanistic movement for social justice but at the same time advocates what she calls the Diane Principle, which "seeks revenge against men." As discussed in the chapter on Samson, this is a distorted view of justice in which Samson, not being complemented with the forgiveness and love aspects of the feminine principle, judges and seeks revenge for perceived wrongs. This hardly seems to me to be an advance forward in the actualization of the feminine principle or a totally new direction for feminism.

Can feminism truly take a new direction in the 2020's: (1) one that accepts diversity and individual development; (2) one that offers different views on the nature of femininity— psychological vs. sociological; and (3) one that extends the feminine principle into the world. The paradigm presented in this book suggests a new direction that incorporates each of these three characteristics. In terms of the first characteristic, it is inclusive and accepting and not divisive and rejecting. The "gender" feminists of the second wave were rather totalitarian and dictatorial in their views on the nature of femininity and which aspects should be expressed in the world. However, these second wave feminists did do a good job of helping women become aware of how they had unconsciously identified with the roles projected onto to them by the culture as well as furthering such equity issues as pay and benefits. These first steps were important because in order to change one's thinking and then one's behavior it's necessary to first become aware of its existence. However, their views today, thirty years after the sixties, have become more rigid, narrow, and attacking. This can be seen in the *Revolution from Within* by Gloria Steinem which centers on attacking and condemning the patriarchal culture and men in general. Although Wolf in her book *Fire with Fire* states the need for the women's movement to accept the diversity of expression of the feminine principle and to stop blaming men for all of their problems, there are still large components of gender feminists thinking there. She wanted feminism in the 1990's to be focused on women gaining power but still talks about "political retribution for an insult to the sex." The paradigm in this book recognizes Wolf's work as focusing on the power issues of Samson but believes the real work of dealing with power lies inside of a woman on a psychological level. It also recognizes that many women may be dealing with issues regarding their femininity and masculinity that lie in areas other than power. They may be dealing with issues revolving around their other inner men—David, Paul or Jesus.

The paradigm suggested in this book is inclusive and accepting. It recognizes that women are at different stages in their masculine/feminine development. It does not judge or condemn any particular path of individuation that a woman is walking down nor how far along the path she has traveled. The focus is not on condemning the masculine in men but praising it in women. Nor is the focus on calling women to identify with this part of themselves and become a pseudoman. This is hardly the fully actualized state of a woman.

The new direction or wave proposed here is a psychological/spiritual one emphasizing the wholistic development of a woman. This direction recognizes that the real work of femininity is inside of a woman. It lies in the transformation of the negative masculine within a woman, which dampens, blocks, and distorts the true expression of her femininity. The past focus in feminism has been more sociological than psychological. Gloria Steinem and many second wave feminists performed an important function of helping women become aware of their unconscious cultural conditioning about femininity. However, the resolutions that they proposed to escape the conditioning further enslaved women or turn them away from identification with the feminist movement. They were and are not aware that undoing the negative masculine begins inside of themselves. They are unaware that they have projected their negative inner men outward onto the culture. They then were and are now trying to correct and change their inner men on the outside at a cultural level rather than inside on a psychological level.

Now that we as women have become aware of how we have unconsciously identified with certain patriarchal notions of femininity projected on to us the next step is to correct it inside of our own minds. We also need to examine how our inner masculine side may be functioning negatively and preventing the actualization and extension of our feminine principle. We then need to project the new femininity found inside of ourselves outward into the culture. In this way the old inappropriate models of femininity can come tumbling down. We simply don't identify with them; instead, we actualize and extend the feminine in ourselves. As discussed earlier, it may range from such diverse forms as the mother of children to the mother of ideas or of a nation. But whatever form is dominant within oneself that needs to be accepted inside by a woman herself as well as outside by other women. It's hardly helpful to have feminists attack or judge as inferior the true expression of one's femininity. This approach would seem to be more of a revolution within than that discussed by Gloria Steinem.

The next wave of feminism emphasized the extension of the feminine principle into the world to complement the masculine that's already there. Marianne Williamson also called women to extend the feminine principle into the world:

> A woman is meant to hold the heart of the world within her hands. She must cater to it and minister to it and kiss it when it cries. We are meant to keep the home fires burning, the fires in our hearts. We are meant to prepare the food, the spiritual food of love and compassion. We are meant to care for the children, not just our own, but every child. When we do not recognize our cosmic function, our own hearts break, and so does the heart of the world.

Unlike many second wave "gender" feminists, the mission here is not one of blame and shame or attack and destroy directed at the patriarchal aspect of the culture and its institutions. Rather, the mission is one of extension of the feminine principle and of joining with the masculine principle. Christianity as the traditional religious institution has come under attack by feminists. Many second wave "gender" feminists have left Christianity, which they consider to be male- dominated and sexist. Believing that Christianity is solely for men and designed by men, some feminists have resurrected the rituals and returned to worshipping goddesses and mother goddess myths. Gloria Steinem even maintains that "monotheism is but imperialism in religion." She reflects, "Why should we worship a male-only god who makes women feel ungodly, and men feel they must be godlike?" She believes that fundamentalism appeals to women because "the promise is safety in return for obedience, respectability in return for self-respect and freedom—a sad bargain." She suggests that, "discovering pre-patriarchal myths and holy places as well as the still living pagan beliefs of many indigenous cultures and mystical traditions" would give back "a universal spirituality."

Instead of totally rejecting Christianity or throwing the baby out with the bath water, why not extend and shine the light of consciousness on the feminine that's already there? How can going backward in time to earlier ways of religious thinking be a revolutionary step forward? It would seem to me that a true revolution would be one in which the feminine in Christianity is brought out of the shadows of the masculine to join in a conscious complementary relationship of wholeness.

As stated earlier in this book, I believe that Jesus brought the feminine aspect of God, the heart of God, to balance with the masculine or head of God that was revealed to Moses during Old Testament times. The main themes that Jesus talked about were love and forgiveness, two major aspects based on the feminine principle. One of the main reasons why I chose to use Christian images in this book was to help women see that the feminine principle is actually the core of Christianity. As stated earlier, Jesus revealed His greatest truths to women and at a time when such discussions with women were unheard of.

Yes, Christianity has been dominated by men, but we as women have a responsibility to extend and stand for the feminine there, not return to earlier less evolved ways of spiritual thinking. Maybe we need to question ourselves as to why we allowed the masculine to overshadow the feminine heart of God that Jesus brought rather than simply blame men for this. As Marianne Williamson stated, "it's time to remember we're the daughters of God."

Another institution that needs to be complemented with the feminine principle as an equal and valid partner is that of marriage. The traditional views of marriage in this culture are based primarily on the Christian writings of Paul. This has resulted in a male power/domination view of superiority and inferiority in the marital relationship rather than egalitarian one. They have also resulted in the concept of helpmate being associated primarily with women rather than with men. Needless to say, feminists have attacked this patriarchal view without fully recognizing the real importance of the marital relationship in the psychological/spiritual development of a woman.

Previous chapters have already discussed reinterpretations of biblical scriptures that suggest that the marital relationship is egalitarian and really a partnership between a man and a woman. But let's explore further the idea of helpmate. Although helpmate has traditionally been applied to women, it also applies to men in the marital relationship. In the present focus, the lens is centered on the concept of helpmate from a psychological/spiritual vantage point. That is, how both a man and a woman are helpmates to each other in their psychological/spiritual development. The marriage thus becomes a classroom for the development of wholeness within each partner.

As stated earlier in this book, men identify with their masculinity by rejecting and repressing their feminine side. Their masculinity thus hinges on the rejection of their feminine side. Women identify with their femininity on a conscious level and repress their masculine side. Gloria

Steinem recognizes that each of us has both masculine and feminine sides but she fails to see that one's inner development causes them to fragment these two parts. She again blames the patriarchal culture for this split. She maintains that our basic nature is "both masculine and feminine" but our patriarchal and gender-polarized culture forces us to identify with a gender role. We then "project life-giving parts ... onto another human being and believe we can find ourselves in a foreign substance; that is, in the body and mind of another person." She views this form of relationship as negative and being brought on by a male-dominated culture rather than a phase in a woman's psychological/spiritual development.

When a man and a woman fall in love, they do project their split-off contrasexual nature onto each other. That is, the "romance"—to use Steinem's word—or the love-at-first-sight phenomenon that occurs between a man and a woman is one of unconscious projections. Steinem considers this to be a conspiracy perpetuated by our male-dominated culture. The present psychological/spiritual model of feminism, however, sees the relationship between a man and a woman as a classroom for the development of each person's wholeness. The woman serves as a helpmate to teach her man about his repressed and projected feminine side so that he can assimilate it into consciousness and complete his wholeness. However, a man is also a helpmate to a woman to teach her about her repressed and projected masculine side so that she can assimilate him into consciousness and complete her wholeness. Thus, with the idea of both a man and a woman serving as helpmates to each other in an equal partnership, a classroom of wholeness results rather than a battleground of anger and attack between the sexes. This classroom could help both a man and a woman integrate their contrasexual nature and bring about a new psychological/spiritual level of development. As Marianne Williamson stated:

> We have the opportunity to forge a marriage between
> masculine and feminine, more potent and more vibrant

than any we have experienced on the earth for ages —
more beautiful, perhaps, than any the earth has ever
known

This new level of development can then be projected into the culture
and new traditions can be established which reflect the union of the
masculine and feminine principles. Such a revolution is far different from
what has been seen and suggested by second wave "gender" feminists.

Now we have come full circle from femininity to masculinity and
back to femininity. Like the mysterious woman appearing in St. John's
revelation at the end of time, to be truly feminine, is to stand on the moon
clothed with the sun—to use our inner man to serve the feminine, to
extend the feminine into the world where it is so sorely needed to balance
the masculine. It's interesting that both times that Christ appears in the
Bible we see such a woman. First there's Mary, who was fully balanced and
used her inner men to further the full expression of the feminine, and then
there's the woman at the end of time who is associated with the second
coming of Christ. Maybe Baal Shan was right when he said, "When the
moon shines as bright as the son, the Messiah will come." That is, when
we have integrated our masculine and feminine aspects into a balanced
relationship we will become whole again.

BIBLIOGRAPHY

Beasley, Chris. *What is Feminism?* New York: Sage, 1995.

Castillejo, Irene. *Knowing Woman*. New York: Harper & Row Publishers, 1981.

Chamberlain, Prudence. *The Feminist Fourth Wave: Affective Temporality*. Palgrave Macmillan, 2017.

Dychtwald, Ken. *Bodymind*. New York: Jove Publications, 1977.

Guillaumont, A., H. Puech, W. Quispel and A. Yassah. *The Gospel According to St. Thomas.* New York: Harper & Row Publishers, 1959.

Dart. John. "Eve's Helpmate Status Disputed". *Times Herald Dallas*: February 23, 1983.

Este's, Clarissa Pinkola. *Women Who Run with Wolves*. New York: Ballantine Books, 1992

Fox, Margalit (5 February 2006). *"Betty Friedan, Who Ignited Cause in Feminine Mystic,"* *The New York Times. Retrieved 19 February 2017*.

Hannah, Barbara. *Striving Towards Wholeness*. New York: C.G. Jung Foundation, 1971.

Harding, Esther. *Women's Mysteries, Ancient and Modern*. New York: Harper & Row Publishers, 1976.

Humm, Maggie. *The Dictionary of Feminist Theory*. Columbus: Ohio State University Press, 1995.

Jung, Carl. *Mam and His Symbols*. Garden City, New York: Doubleday, 1964.

Jung, Emma. *Animus and Anima*. Zurich: Spring Publications, 1974.

Keith, Lierre &Jensen, Derrick. *"The Emperor's New Penis"*. *Counterpunch*. Retrieved 27 August 2014.

Kluger, Rivkah. *Psyche and the Bible*. Zurich: Spring Publications, 1974.

Krolokke, Charlotte & Scott, Anne. *"Three Waves of Feminism: From Suffragettes to Girls" Gender Communication Theories and Analyses: From Silence to Performance*. Sage, 2005.

Leonard, Linda. *The Wounded Woman: Healing the Father-Daughter Relationship*. Boulder, Colorado: Shambhala Publications, 1982.

Morgan, Marabel. *The Total Woman*. Old Tappan, N.J: Fleming H. Revell Company, 1973.

Mosbacher, Georgette. *Feminine Force*. New York: Fireside, 1994.

Neuman, Erich. *The Great Mother*. Princeton: Princeton University Press, 1963.

Project Gutenberg eBook of the King James Bible, *The King James Bible*, 1989.

Robinson, James (ed.) *The Nag Hammadi Library*. New York: Harper & Row, 1981.

Reuther, Rosemary Radford (2012). *Women and Redemption: A Theological History* (2nd ed.). Minneapolis: Fortress Press, 2012. pp. 112–18, 136–39.

Steinem, Gloria. *Revolution from Within: A Book of Self-Esteem*. Boston: Little, Brown and Company, 1992.

Sommers, Christina Hoff. *Who Stole Feminism? How Women Have Betrayed Women*. New York: Simon & Schuster, 1994.

Ulanov, Ann. *The Feminine in Jungian Psychology and Christian Theology.* Evanston, Illinois: Northwestern Press, 1971.

Valentis, Mary and Anne Devane. *Female Rage: Unlocking its Secrets, Claiming Its Power.* New York: Carol Southern Books, 1994.

Walker, Rebecca (January-February 1992). "Becoming the Third Wave".

Whitmont, Edward. *The Symbolic Quest.* Princeton, New Jersey: Princeton University Press, 1978.

Williamson, Marianne. *A Woman's Worth.* New York: Ballantine Books, 1993.

Wolf, Naomi. *The Beauty Myth: How Images of Beauty are Used Against Women.* New York: William Morrow & Company, 1991.

Wolf, Naomi. *Fire with Fire: The New Female Power and How to Use it.* New York: Ballantine Books, 1994.

Wolff. Toni. *Structural Forms of the Feminine Psyche.* Zurich: Privately Printed, 1956.

Printed in the United States
by Baker & Taylor Publisher Services